GROWING A GREAT SUNDAY SCHOOL CLASS

GROWING A GREAT SUNDAY SCHOOL CLASS

Debra Fulghum Bruce
& Robert G. Bruce, Jr.

Abingdon Press / Nashville

GROWING A GREAT SUNDAY SCHOOL CLASS

This book is printed on acid-free, recycled paper.

Library of Congress Cataloging-in-Publication Data

Bruce, Debra Fulghum, 1951-
    Growing a great Sunday school class / Debra Fulghum Bruce & Robert G. Bruce, Jr.
      p.   cm.
    ISBN 0-687-12173-6 (pbk. : alk. paper)
    1. Sunday schools—Growth. I. Bruce, Robert G., 1949-
II. Title.
BV1523.G75B78   1994
268—dc20

93-41810
CIP

94 95 96 97 98 99 00 01 02 03 — 10 9 8 7 6 5 4 3 2 1

MANUFACTURED IN THE UNITED STATES OF AMERICA

To our dear children—Rob, Brittnye, and Ashley.

May the lessons you learn in Sunday school each week

be passed on to your children.

May faith in our Lord Jesus Christ sustain you each day.

Contents

1

Yes, Your Sunday School Can Grow!

Are you tired of coming to church week after week, realizing that very few visitors ever come to your Sunday school class even though you are well prepared? Do you have ideas for creating enthusiasm in your Sunday school class that you think would result in growth, but you just can't motivate others to assist you?

If you have ever wondered, "Why can't my Sunday school class grow?" then read on, because *this book is for you.* It is for teachers, pastors, educators, and interested laypersons in the church. Whether you are trained in the field of Christian education, have a background in teaching, or are thinking about becoming involved in your Sunday school program—this book is for anyone who is interested in Sunday school evangelism and wants to know how it can be done.

This book is about class growth. It is about identifying new prospects for present Sunday school classes, getting an evangelistic commitment from present members, and energizing those who have stopped coming or come infrequently. It is about encouraging members to respond to the church's challenge to go into all the world and teach the gospel message. This book will show you how to publicize your class, how to be creative in your teaching methods so that members will respond enthusiastically, and how to start new classes so that the message of Jesus Christ can touch more lives.

This book is about energetic evangelism. Your class leadership team will become enthusiastic as you radiate the love of Jesus Christ. Crucial to a growing Sunday school class are evangelistic adults, teens, and children who approach Christ's ministry with energy and a positive sense of adventure. With creative "twists" for lessons, closer relationships among those in the class, a plan for reaching out to those in the community, and enthusiastic teaching, your Sunday school class can experience new ways of being "filled with God."

This book is about caring for all God's people. The gospel message affirms that God loved us so much that God gave us Jesus Christ. Jesus lived a life full of love and caring for everyone. Because of this love, we are free to care for others. As we become ambassadors for Christ, we also mirror God's ever-present grace.

Most people attend the Sunday school class for fellowship. Not only do members receive nurture and training, but Sunday school classes also provide small groups where caring and fellowship is experienced. New Testament Christians called this fellowship *koinonia.* On the same note, many people leave Sunday school classes because of lack of caring and fellowship. One woman shared, "No one was friendly, so why return?" Another young man said, "I never felt important in my class." A child reported: "My class was so big that my teacher did not know my name."

This book will give you and your students a plan of action for Sunday school growth. It offers you an easy-to-read and practical guide with suggestions you can use immediately. In this book, we will share the years of experiences we have gathered in the local church and the wisdom that other pastors, educators, and classroom teachers have shared with us in workshops around the country. Rather than expound on the many theories behind Sunday school growth, this book will teach you how to develop a mind-set for growth: how to take the necessary steps that can really work for Sunday school class growth. These include:

1. Develop an attitude for Sunday school growth.

Your attitude sets the tone for your growth campaign. A positive, winning attitude goes far in motivating those around you to reach out and invite. Paul teaches us to handle conflicts and negative feelings in a positive way: "As God's chosen ones, holy and beloved, clothe yourselves with compassion, kindness, humility, meekness, and patience. Bear with one another and, if anyone has a complaint against another, forgive each other; just as the Lord has forgiven you, so you also must forgive.

> *Above all, clothe*
> *yourselves with love,*
> *which binds everything*
> *together in perfect*
> *harmony." (Col. 3:12-14)*

Your outlook on the Sunday school and its place in the church will ultimately affect your performance. If your attitude is negative, chances are the attitudes of others will be the same.

2. Set goals for a growing report.

Goals are helpful for anyone involved in the Sunday school program—pastors, educators, teachers—for they help turn hopes and dreams into purpose and reality. Without specific goals, you have no guideline by which to measure growth—qualitative or quantitative. Setting goals helps you when attendance declines or when enthusiasm for the class subsides. Goals can help you stay focused on what is most important—touching lives with the gospel message.

3. Organize to touch lives.

Reaching out to inactive members and visitors doesn't happen by chance. Having a growing Sunday school class takes some strategic planning. You can make these plans with your evangelism team, which we call a CARE team. The CARE team is composed of the teacher and interested members of the class who want to work on Sunday school growth. (See page 41 for information on how to start a CARE team.) Record keeping is important as you prepare to reach out beyond your church membership. Tools as simple as a three-by-five-inch file box, creative bulletin boards, a class directory, and personal letters help you make an impression on each person who visits your class.

4. Activate the current membership as you invite persons to the class.

The church is made up of people. And the life of every person is ultimately in the hands of each of us—to strengthen, to nurture, to affirm. Yet, often we become negligent in our responsibilities as "people" builders. "Who has the time to call and invite class members?" a busy woman asked at a teacher's retreat. "I work full-time, raise two teenagers, and barely make it to teach my class on Sunday. I honestly can't do any more."

But we must do more! On every class roll, there are inactive members just waiting to be invited "back" to class. There are unchurched men, women, and children staying home on Sunday morning who could fill your classroom—IF someone invited them. What if no visitors ever came to your class, but you activated everyone on the roll? Many Sunday school classes could double or triple in attendance if they could just activate their current enrollment.

5. Start new classes.

If you want your Sunday school to grow, then start a new class. New classes offer more leaders the chance to touch more lives. New Sunday school classes must be initiated to involve more people in learning God's Word. As more adults are trained to teach these classes, personal caring takes place, bringing these inactive members into the fellowship of the church.

6. Publicize your program through the church and community.

For thirty years or more the Committee on Religion in American Life (RIAL) has done an excellent job of keeping the American public aware of the importance of religion in the life of the nation. Using newspapers, magazines, radio, and television, the committee worked with the Advertising Council to get its message across.

The Great Commission challenges, "Go into all the world and proclaim the good news to the whole creation" (Mark 16:15). An active publicity campaign, using various media, accepts this challenge to reach believers and nonbelievers. Publicity is vital so others can know what your Sunday school class has to offer. Much publicity can be free and effective, if you know who it is for, what you want to say, and how you want to say it.

7. Choose methods that are creative.

Creativity for the 1990s is a necessity! Creativity means reaching out beyond your denomination's curriculum and complementing this with props, innovative methods of teaching, and resource speakers.

8. Reach people where they are in their lives.

This involves visitation on the turf of the student—in the home, at school, at work, or meeting students for lunch during the week. One of the biggest stumbling blocks in the local church is not enough people willing to act as evangelists. We hesitate to make home visits or telephone calls for varied reasons—insecurity, lack of time, or just sheer apathy. Yet everyone has some type of faith story to share. As your team members are encouraged to take the risk of getting to know new, inactive, or shut-in members, caring takes place. And the Sunday school classes that are growing—spiritually and numerically—are usually the ones where outreach is taking place. As lives are touched, inactive members come back into the fold, and new persons feel genuine concern, your team can see the reward of living the Christian faith as shepherds.

9. Provide nurture in the Sunday school.

Bible study, prayer, sharing of joys and concerns, and personal testimony are important in the Sunday school class. Each teacher is challenged to create an environment in the classroom where God's grace can be experienced. Sunday school classes that are evangelistic and that radiate an "owned faith" publicly combine actions and words as team members let the love of Christ move through them into the life of the other.

10. Activate members through fellowship opportunities.

Class socials, theme parties, regular potluck dinners, and weekend retreats are ways your class members can grow close as a group. When members in Sunday school classes take time to recreate and play together, they can make new discoveries about self and others. This fellowship is vital for personal and group growth. Regular times of recreation and togetherness offer class members a chance to develop a sense of belonging—besides the hurried hour on Sunday morning. Members can share personal hobbies and talents as they engage in casual small talk. And recreation on a regular basis can take the stuffiness out of Christian faith as the ice is broken. Sunday school growth can occur when people feel comfortable confiding their sufferings, concerns, goals, and joys with trusted friends from their Sunday school class.

This friendship developed through fellowship is a sign of Sunday school success. "Most successful Sunday school classes are more than just a group of people who want to study the faith together. Research has shown that in many classes a significant percentage of the member's best personal friends are also members of that class (Lyle E. Schaller, ed., *The Parish Paper* [Yokefellow Institute, March 1974]). In fact, it is through the life of the class that their friendships ripen into lasting bonds" (Dick Murray, *Strengthening the Adult Sunday School Class* [Nashville: Abingdon Press, 1981], p. 67).

But these activities take planning and follow-through.

11. Enthusiastically touch lives.

Enthusiasm. It's vital to evangelizing the church today, and it depends on the team—pastors, educators, teachers. That leaves many people asking, "How can I be enthusiastic?"

Let's go back to the original meaning of the word *enthusiasm* ("filled with God"). That doesn't mean being "pious." Rather, it does mean "being full" of God's attitudes—toward yourself, others, classroom goals, and changes that may occur.

12

Your Sunday school team can become enthusiastic if they work to be:

- genuine and honest
- secure in faith and self-image
- good listeners
- positive and affirming
- fun to be around

These are all qualities that can be developed.

An enthusiastic and growing Sunday school class will experience God's abundant love as it reaches out to others.

Finally, this book is about challenge. The Bible challenges Christians to be evangelistic—to know one another's names and care for one another. In John 10:3*b*, we find, "And the sheep hear his voice. He calls his own sheep by name and leads them out." Can't you picture the worn shepherd keeping track of all the furry sheep, large and small, young and old, as they enter the pasture for grazing? Most shepherds verify that if one sheep becomes lost or hurt along the way, they will leave the flock to go comfort it.

As teachers and leaders in Christ's church, we are called upon to be shepherds. We are commissioned to teach the Word of God, as we work to heal the wounds, celebrate the victories, and provide opportunities for response for our students.

Christ believed in the principle that a small group of well-trained disciples could permeate a larger group in much the same way that a little yeast in the dough leavens the whole loaf (Luke 13:21). Jesus not only taught this principle, he also put it into practice in the training of the Twelve. It was through the investment of himself in an intimate, instructive, purposeful relationship that Jesus equipped the apostles. Through the course of a few years, he trained them by indelibly stamping their lives with a model of ministry they could not forget (Win Arn, ed., *The Pastor's Church Growth Handbook* [Pasadena, Calif.: Church Growth Press, 1979], p. 29).

As leaders and teachers in the Sunday school, we must also indelibly stamp lives within our classrooms, our church, and our community. Our concern for others must be so intimate, so full of selfless love, that people know we are authentic. "You yourselves have been taught by God to love one another" (1 Thess. 4:9*b*).

Jesus' final emphasis in his ministry is to "go . . . and make disciples of all nations . . . teaching them" (Matt. 28:18-20). Jesus' commandment begins with our personal witness in the classroom as we teach to share information and teach for a gracious confrontation; providing that classroom environment where grace can be experienced and an "owned" faith is the expected result.

Triumph. Success. These two celebration words go hand in hand. As you work with your team—pastors, educators, teachers, and students—you can carefully and prayerfully attempt to build your Sunday school class. The triumph and success will be yours as more lives are touched by our Lord.

2

Start with a Winning Attitude

Susan, a youth teacher in a small congregation, cannot understand why her students are frequently absent. "I get so upset at their lack of commitment that I rarely smile during the lesson," she said with bitterness. "They know I don't like it when they aren't regular in their attendance. How can I plan effectively?"

The sad note is that Susan's negative attitude has influenced the behavior of her class members.

How about you? How is your attitude toward the members of your class? Toward your responsibility as a teacher? Did you know that what you say or how you act and react has a great influence on those around you?

Perhaps a self-attitude check would help give more insight. (See page 16.)

How did you score? If you chose the "yes" blanks, then your attitude is probably up to par. If you didn't, read on!

Attitudes can determine the success or failure of a Sunday school class. And becoming motivated for Sunday school growth begins with the right attitude. You have encountered persons who radiate enthusiasm or a positive attitude. This person can enter into a negative situation and motivate a positive response with their leadership and guidance.

Take Bill, for instance. Bill was a senior in college when he taught the middle school students at our church. Even though he worked part-time and had a heavy academic load in college, Bill cared enough for these early teens to be there each week, without exception. He was always well prepared with a lesson and discussion that related to these early teens. And Bill was always smiling; he knew each child's name. Now that was important! Yes, Bill had the right attitude for teaching Sunday school and touched many young lives in our church and community as his class was filled with members and visitors each week.

15

Attitude Check for Teachers

Check the appropriate blank for each statement.

YES/NO

___ ___ Whether I have one student or many students, I continue teaching my lesson with enthusiasm each week.

___ ___ If attendance has been down for several Sundays, I work even harder at being creative in my teaching methods.

___ ___ When a student has been absent for awhile, I make a personal home visit to see if there are problems.

___ ___ If the students seem distracted or uninterested in the lesson, I evaluate my teaching methods to see how changes might be made.

___ ___ The commitment I initially made for teaching is still strong, and I never feel apathy toward my mission in the church.

___ ___ I enjoy all classroom responsibilities such as making creative crafts, taking the roll, and cleanup at the end of the session.

___ ___ When I have to do something I don't want to do in the classroom or church, I don't complain to others.

___ ___ If someone or something interrupts my lessons or plans, I adjust and remain flexible in my routine.

___ ___ My students and other church members know I am a committed Christian by my enthusiasm for Christ and for life.

___ ___ When a student or other church member makes a suggestion about my class or teaching methods, I listen willingly.

___ ___ I look forward to teaching my class and creating a classroom environment where God's grace can be experienced.

___ ___ If I have a difficult student, I try to find ways to work with this person instead of ignoring him or her.

___ ___ I have the same attitude toward life at work, at play, and in the classroom.

___ ___ I never blame the church, class members, or the pastor for difficulties I may experience in my life.

Is having the right attitude or being a teacher who attracts others to the Sunday school that important today? According to Dick Murray, the teacher is 90 percent of the teaching/learning equation. In other words, in our pursuit of life, we do not follow ideas—we follow people. "When God wanted to fully reveal himself he came *in a person*, and we know God through that person (Jesus Christ) and many other persons. *Personality is an asset, not a liability*" (Dick Murray, *Strengthening the Adult Sunday School Class* [Nashville: Abingdon Press, 1981], p. 78).

Many Christians admit to "following" a certain pastor or teacher if given a choice. Julie, a pediatrician with four young children, said, "I am on call at the hospital many Sunday mornings, so I have to plan my day in order to attend my class. I have to admit that my time is limited, and I have chosen the class where I am certain that the teacher cared enough to prepare and who is pleasant to be around."

ENTHUSIASM IS CONTAGIOUS

Now the whole concept of "following" a certain teacher as Julie describes may suggest that we are placing too much emphasis on the class leader and not enough on the material or curriculum. But, like it or not, an enthusiastic teacher is vital to success in the Sunday school. David Seabury said, "Enthusiasm is the best protection in any situation. Wholeheartedness is contagious. Give yourself, if you wish to get others." Yes, whether we like it or not, it is a fact of human nature that people are attracted to people who are strong, genuine, and who possess a winning, spirited attitude.

Can you change your attitude for teaching? For Jesus Christ? Can you be that key person who presents the Word so enthusiastically and with such conviction that members flock to hear you and be with you?

Paul taught us that we are to be of the right attitude all the time. "Don't copy the behavior and customs of this world, but be a new and different person with a fresh newness in all you do and think. Then you will learn from your own experience how his ways will really satisfy you" (Rom. 12:2 TLB).

RENEW YOUR COMMITMENT TO TEACHING

To catch that "fresh newness" Paul speaks of, that winning spirit, you must first reevaluate your commitment to teaching. Why did you become a teacher? Try to remember the moment in your life when you said "yes" to teaching in Christ's church.

- Do you remember the drive and enthusiasm you had at that moment?
- Who asked you to teach?
- Did you volunteer out of a special calling or need to serve?

To keep that zest and vitality so necessary for teaching, it is important to look back at the very reasons that brought you into the classroom. Nancy, a teacher for ten years, said, "I remember being so moved one Sunday morning by our pastor's sermon on putting 'Feet to Faith.' I had been attending a large adult class and had felt the need for a new class. After Pastor Glenn's sermon, I made an appointment with him and committed myself to teaching. I've been teaching an adult discussion class ever since."

Another second grade teacher explained, "Every summer I take two weeks off from teaching to go on vacation and reevaluate my teaching commitment. Without fail, by the end of my vacation, I cannot wait to get back to my class. I miss my students, their laughter, and the personal growth I witness each week. There is something contagious about the students' spirit that adds meaning to my life. I know God put me there for a reason."

Whatever sparked your commitment to teach, take time now to remember the emotions and thoughts you first had when you said "yes." Say aloud, "I am a teacher in Christ's church. I am a Sunday school teacher." Believe in your God-given talents, and daily ask God to bless your ministry in the Sunday school classroom. Ask your pastor and other teachers to pray for your commitment, and with God's help, renew your teaching vow as you continue with new purpose each week.

> *"I am a teacher*
> *in Christ's church.*
> *I am a Sunday school*
> *teacher."*

REFLECT ON CHILDHOOD DAYS

Think back to your childhood days. Do you remember the first Christian who had a tremendous influence in your life? This person was probably someone who made you feel loved, who made you want to learn what they knew, and who brought out the best in you. Chances are this person was your Sunday school teacher!

What did this Christian do that made him or her so impressive in your life? Was it his or her attitude toward you? Did this special person believe in you? Affirm you? Care for you? Encourage you? It is amazing how many of these descriptions of the first Christians who touched our lives look like a powerful example of the incarnate love of Christ.

Thank God that someone cared enough to share the love of Christ with us! The Sunday school teacher who enthusiastically leads in the classroom combines actions and words as he or she lets the love of Christ move into the life of the other.

Personal evangelism through telling of the faith in the classroom is difficult. Some teachers struggle even thinking about sharing their faith, and even the most gregarious teachers may become tongue-tied when asked to speak in personal terms about their faith. A friend said, "I could never teach Sunday school! I am so afraid that if I tell someone about my relationship with God they will ask me a biblical question I don't know, then I really won't be an effective witness. And besides that, I would be totally embarrassed. What if someone in the class knew more about the Bible?"

But personal evangelism and witnessing are part of living a Christian life. In Acts 1:8, Jesus spoke about witnessing using plain and simple words, saying "you will receive power when the Holy Spirit has come upon you; and you will be my witnesses. . . ." And in 2 Corinthians 5:20, Paul explains, "So we are ambassadors for Christ, since God is making his appeal through us."

As Sunday school teachers, we may be the "best" Christians our students know. Realizing this, it seems all the more vital that our students experience the peace and joy that Christ brings to all of our lives as they enter the classroom on Sunday morning. Our challenge is to continue the two-thousand-year legacy of the Christian faith by sharing with those in our class *and* inviting others to join us as we become a growing Sunday school class.

REDEDICATE YOUR TALENTS, ABILITIES, AND ATTITUDE

To be this enthusiastic person in the Sunday school, the classroom teacher must rededicate her or his time, gifts, and attitude every day. Try following these guidelines:

1. Always come prepared for teaching and touching lives with Christ's gospel message.

Spend at least one hour a week in prayer and preparation before each Sunday's lesson. Each week, write down your lesson plans and ideas. Set classroom goals, collect supplies, and organize your thoughts. Allow time to pray and meditate about the lesson and class members' needs. Make a commitment to be in the classroom at least twenty minutes before the first student arrives. This will let class members know that you care enough to lead the way instead of hurriedly coming in late. This extra morning time on Sunday will also give you a few moments to collect your thoughts, pray, and relax before you begin your teaching.

2. Make a special effort to know everyone in the classroom, including your visitors and inactive members.

Talk with the students outside the classroom, invite them to your home, and visit their homes. Find out their needs, their faith struggles, their goals and weaknesses. By involving yourself personally with each student, relationships begin to form, making it easier to communicate the message of the gospel and your own faith experience.

Response is the key to teaching, and response takes time. Without it, however, you will never know if learning has taken place.

3. Recruit assistance with your class.

As you work on a winning attitude, delegate classroom responsibilities to others in the class. If your time is limited, ask a member or other adult helper to keep the class roster and follow through on absentees. Other members might assist with minor details such as straightening the classroom, moving chairs, passing out papers, and so on.

Todd, an adult class teacher, told of sharing all classroom responsibilities. "Our class functions quite well by having officers handle all duties not directly related to presenting the lesson. Each Sunday morning, the president leads the business section of the session, the vice-president takes the roll and follows up on absentees, the secretary keeps a record of all decisions, and the treasurer takes the offering and handles other funds. I teach at the end of the business portion."

Never be afraid to ask others for help in your teaching. Call your pastor or superintendent if you have questions regarding the material.

Chris commented that after teaching third grade for five years, he was finally feeling comfortable. "I had taught for five years straight without admitting that I had questions. I didn't want to appear ignorant, but as I asked for assistance from others, I realized that these other teachers and staff persons were human too. Often they needed help with a question or class problem. I even called the editor of my curriculum, and we discussed the meaning of the lesson on the phone. I felt good inside after I sought help, and my children profited."

Remember, you can't do it all alone. Recruit help, ask questions, and seek answers before you feel overwhelmed.

4. Really listen to your students.

"Be still, and know that I am God" (Ps. 46:10*a*). Listening is a vital part of our faith. We need to hear God's response to our prayers. But the Sunday school teacher who attracts class members must also listen to students' reactions to the Scriptures, their interpretations of the lessons, and their interaction in the classroom. As you take time to listen to each person's story, you will learn how to better guide the entire class.

Jesus exhibited listening skills as he patiently dealt with people and problems each day. The Bible, in fact, has much to say about communication. In John 8:1-11, Jesus patiently listened to the scribes and Pharisees as they accused a woman of committing adultery. He spoke kind words to her, and solved the problem presented to him without harsh punishment. Other similar events share the same gospel message: Jesus listened intently to the problem before responding in love.

5. Be a genuine witness to God's unconditional love.

Share your life with your students. Talk with them about faith and how God moves in your life. Listen to their prayer concerns and keep these in mind as you pray each day. As a teacher in the Sunday school classroom, think of yourself as a stationary planet with many satellites revolving around you. Your students see you as an example to follow, so you must take time to set the example in the Sunday school classroom by respecting each individual, dealing with personal and group conflicts, and living a life according to Jesus' teachings.

6. Look beyond the curriculum being taught and use innovative ideas to reach students.

Creativity in relating the Bible to life in the 1990s is vital. Search for resources to complement the lesson each week. Chapter 8 tells of using teaching aids, such as props, filmstrips, recordings, charts, costumes, and other creative touches to enhance your lesson. Locate professionals in your church or community who can speak on topics concerning your lesson. Purchase or borrow suggested curriculum resources.

7. Provide an environment in the classroom where God's grace can be shared and faith is the result.

Let your students feel comfortable in expressing emotions, concerns, personal joys, and frustrations without fear of being ridiculed. You can provide such a secure atmosphere in your class where feelings can be expressed by leading the way. During times of class interaction and discussion, interject your own personal history. Tell of struggles you had as a child, a teen, and an adult. Tell how God helped you cope with crises or disappointments. Mention how you felt in the situation—afraid, nervous, empty. Talk about your emotions in terms your students can understand—the pounding heart that accompanies being afraid or nervous; the pain in the stomach that goes with loneliness; the dull feeling that goes with mild depression.

As you risk being open and talk about your life struggles as a Christian, your students will begin to trust you and feel comfortable enough to express their feelings within the safety of the Sunday school class.

8. Make contact with the class members during the week.

Take a few minutes each day to touch base with several students. You might allow a period during the evening to talk with students on the phone or make a point to meet a student during the week. Talk about the person's interests, and listen! Find out what bothers them, what they dream about, and what they fear. Go further and read between the lines. Does the student appear to talk "big" but seem lonely and scared inside? Does he lack confidence in himself? These insights are important since they give clues to behavior and help you handle discipline problems that may occur on Sunday morning.

Send notes (on personal stationery) to students who are absent on Sunday morning, or send a card to affirm someone who reached out to another or participated in the class discussion. Sometimes, calling all students in your class to tell them of a change in the lesson plan, to encourage them to do well during the week or simply to say you are thinking of them brings a true friendship bond between you and the student. (Chapter 4 offers more innovative ideas on how to keep in touch with students each week.)

9. Believe in the worth of each student.

"A friend loves at all times, and kinsfolk are born to share adversity" (Prov. 17:17). As the Sunday school teacher, you are the liaison between your class and the church, between your students and the family. If you sense a problem with a student, seek help with your pastor. If you see apathy toward the student by other class members, work as his or her ally and help to boost class support and the student's morale.

A teacher with a winning attitude is loyal and takes risks in supporting his or her students. These students, on the other hand, become faithful to the teacher and show their faithfulness in class attendance and response.

10. Know when to get a substitute.

A teacher with a winning attitude knows the symptoms of burnout. And most winning teachers realize teacher burnout as they thrive on dedication, extra caring, and commitment.

Take time out when you become too negative or critical of the students in your class. Jesus set a good example for us when he retreated to be alone with God. When he prayed and meditated on the hillside, he put aside daily concerns and asked God for new power for living. This time out renewed his spirit and enabled him to live out his ministry.

For the Sunday school teacher who sees his or her enthusiasm waning, a substitute teacher and weekend off may be just the remedy for the problem.

Your teaching expectations and attitude can determine the response of your students. If you are excited about the gospel message and concerned about each class member, you will radiate joy. Students will want to be near you and learn from you. As you become more aware of the attributes of having a winning attitude in the Sunday school classroom, you can use these techniques each week.

Yes, our Lord is alive in the personal setting of the Sunday school classroom! With the right attitude, the Sunday school teacher's responsibility is to relay this marvelous message to all.

3

Set Goals for a Growing Report

Perhaps you are beginning to understand the importance of a winning attitude for Sunday school teachers. But do you still wonder why some classes constantly report increased attendance and enrollment while other classes remain with just the same few members year after year? Perhaps the Sunday school classes that have growing reports are also making time to set goals for Sunday school growth.

For example, in the Koinonia class the members tried for over a year to start a young adult class but had only three couples in attendance. "One year is a long time to go without growing," the teacher admitted. "In fact, we were just about ready to disband and spread out into other classes when we decided to give it an aggressive push."

This aggressive push included setting goals for classroom growth. "We realized that wanting to grow and really doing something about it were two different matters," the teacher continued. "In fact, we realized that Sunday school class growth doesn't just happen. We found that it involved goal setting, evangelism, and risking in faith that growth would occur."

In a three-month period, after following through on the classroom goals for growth, this class grew by twenty members. We were witnesses of this growth as founding members of the class. This dramatic increase was just the motivation and success the members needed to continue to invite new people to their class. Today, over fifteen years later, the Koinonia class is one of the strongest and most active groups in the church.

DO YOU REALLY WANT TO GROW?

Often there are classes that do not want to grow with new members. Sometimes the problem is within the class itself because the members like the comfortable feeling of being like "one big, happy family" (or more often, "one small, happy family"). The problem can be with a teacher who feels intimidated with growth and questions, "How could I handle more students? What if they don't like my method of teaching? What if they differ theologically from the other class members?"

If the purpose of the church is to reach all people with the message of salvation, then numbers do become important—not for the sake of "success" but rather to communicate the message of the gospel. Our commitment to growth in our Sunday school must come out of our devotion to Jesus Christ and a dedication to follow his example.

But, in order for a Sunday school to grow, it takes teamwork—the pastor, leaders, teachers, and students *all* motivated for growth. *All of these persons must make a commitment to seek and accept new members.*

In James 2:20, we realize that "faith without works is dead" (KJV). Sunday school growth takes active *goal setting, evangelism, and invitation, then risking in faith* that growth will occur.

GOALS FOR GROWTH

Growth in the Sunday school classroom begins with goal setting. Goals are vital for success. In the local church, setting goals can help turn the dreams of numerical growth into a reality. Without specific goals, you and your leadership team have no guidelines by which to measure growth—quantitative or qualitative.

Frank, an educator from a church in Wisconsin, said that goals were especially helpful for their adult class when attendance became stagnant or when the enthusiasm for evangelism declined. "The members in one class in our church began to evaluate the class goals periodically and were able to determine which changes needed to be made," Frank said. "If there was a drop in attendance for several weeks, that was an immediate 'red flag.' They knew that an effort needed to be made to get members back into the fold."

As you begin to make plans for Sunday school growth, let the following steps assist you in establishing goals:

1. Talk with your members and find out what expectations they have for class growth.

Dream. Brainstorm. Plan. Talk with your class members and visualize your class a year from now. What do you see? Do you want to increase the number of students in your class? Then write down a reasonable number of new members you would like to have. If you need to find new curriculum, a different manner of teaching the lesson, or even move to a new space, picture how this will take place. All your goals and dreams can be a reality if the present leaders, teachers, and students take this on as a challenge.

2. Decide what it would take to make these goals happen.

Remember, faith without works is dead. Meeting your members' goals involves putting some energy into evangelism. This evangelism entails affirming present members each week so that the sense of community is continued. Inactive members must be contacted and encouraged to come back to the Sunday school classes with personal visits, telephone calls, and cards in the mail by you and other concerned class members. And new prospects must be invited to attend your Sunday school so that the rosters can grow.

As you are talking about meeting your class goals, determine WHO will initiate the action, and WHEN and HOW these goals will be met. Again, goal setting is important, but it is the class members who get behind these goals and make sure they happen.

As the Koinonia class began to grow, they found it became important to list on paper the necessary planning steps to reach the specific membership goal. "It was important that specific people in the class became responsible for certain actions each week," the teacher explained. "This helped make sure that the goals were being followed through."

The list of classroom goals they set included:

• Each member (specific people) calls five people from the master list—weekly (how often).
• The class secretary (specific person) sends out direct mail flier telling of the new study, where the class meets, time of class—monthly (how often).
• The CARE team (specific persons) follows up each week with absentees—phone calls or cards in the mail—weekly (how often).
• Members (specific persons) plan class socials, invite, and bring persons off the master list to these parties—monthly (how often).

As members of the class took assignments from list of goals and followed through with the responsibilities, they began to see results.

3. Take time during class each week to review your goals.

The goals your members set give purpose to your Sunday school class each week. Reviewing your goals regularly with your members enables you to see which goals have been reached. The faith of your students will be strengthened as the membership increases.

Warren, a teacher of a large membership class, said, "We use goal setting within our class and this has brought our class together. Before we started goal setting, our class seemed fragmented as members came and went without any concern for class unity. Now the members seem to really care about one another, especially as we go over our 'internal goals' each week. They can see the strengths and weaknesses of our group and work to build one another up."

If you find that someone has neglected his responsibility in following through with a goal, gently remind this person. If he doesn't want the task, ask for another volunteer so the initial growth goal of the class is not hindered.

4. As your class needs change, so must your goals.

Evaluation is important!

If you have succeeded in obtaining your membership growth goals, then spend time and energy on setting new goals for the class—personal caring, fellowship groups, Bible studies, outreach projects, prayer partners, and alternative meeting times are ways in which your CARE team members can extend their energies into developing their faith and really involving these new members in the fellowship of the Sunday school. (See page 41 for information on starting a CARE team in your class.)

Goals do not have to be extravagant. Rather, balance is the key as you aim for emotional, spiritual, academic, and social growth in all students.

SAMPLE GOALS

Here are some sample goals you could set for the Sunday school year as you work to boost enrollment and involvement in your class:

1. Recruit a CARE team.

We speak about the CARE team throughout this book for it is a great benefit to any class that wants to grow. Plan for the CARE team to meet weekly until you feel comfortable that goals are being met. See chapter 5 for ways to train your CARE team.

2. Send out postcards EVERY week to absentees and visitors.

Have a supply of stamped, blank postcards and distribute these to CARE team members. Ask each volunteer to write notes on these cards to any visitor or absentee after Sunday school class, then drop these in the mail.

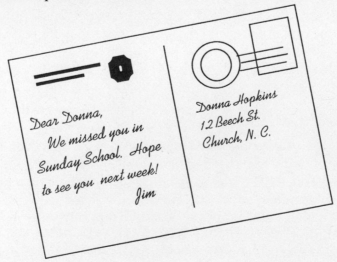

Dear Donna,
We missed you in Sunday School. Hope to see you next week!
Jim

Donna Hopkins
12 Beech St.
Church, N. C.

3. Divide your class roll among the CARE team members and begin personal home visits.

Weekly visits may seem like a duty of the past, but in a time when life is hectic, personal visits are especially meaningful as one feels loved and cared for.

4. Personally contact each visitor either by phone or home visits.

Encourage visitors to return and tell them about other church programs. Seek assistance from the pastor or evangelism committee in your church as you tell newcomers about the total ministry of your congregation.

5. Challenge other teachers in your Sunday school program to a membership drive.

Meet with these teachers regularly so everyone knows what is happening. A membership drive should be based on the percentage of members attending each week, not total attendance.

6. Evaluate results periodically and change direction, if needed.

As you meet with your CARE team, go over the goals. Once goals are met, scratch them off or star them. Add more goals to your list, and be specific!

7. Make the most of publicity opportunities.

Use opportunities during worship, family night suppers, and other intergenerational gatherings to tell about class projects, studies, and upcoming social events. Take advantage of creative means of giving information such as drama, clowning, videos, or slides as you tell the advantages of being part of a Sunday school class.

As you become aware of setting goals for class growth, work through the steps on the "GROWTH" report on the next page and challenge your members with the goal of class growth.

Go through the steps needed for class growth with your team, and check off what your Sunday school class has done to encourage growth recently. Are there any blanks left? If there are, realize that each suggestion is important and recruit volunteers to fill in the black spaces. Encourage your class members to assist in several capacities, either by being a greeter, providing transportation, or making the coffee or juice for fellowship time each week.

Evaluate your current growth status using this list. Do you need to place more focus on creating a welcoming environment in the rooms? Do you need more organization for caring with people in charge of membership or someone from the class in charge of follow-up of visitors each week? Perhaps your members need to work on "inviting" as they take a Saturday to go out as evangelism teams calling on unchurched friends and inviting them to class. Whatever the needs your class has, make sure that some person will pick up on these needs and follow through.

Robert Schuller has warned, "If you fail to plan, you plan to fail." Planning is vital for growth in the Sunday school, and steps for growth must be adhered to. Growth happens in those Sunday school classes where leaders make time to evaluate their strengths and weaknesses, then take steps to invite others to get involved in their fellowship.

Sunday School GROWTH Report

NEEDS FOR GROWTH **RESPONSIBLE PERSON**

A growing Sunday school needs:

_____Clean classrooms with enough chairs for all members and empty chairs for visitors

_____Chairs arranged in an inviting manner, in a circle or around a table, so no one is excluded

_____Tables straightened, bookshelves cleaned, a welcoming environment for guests

_____Designated person, perhaps the teacher, who arrives at least twenty minutes early to greet early arrivals

_____Name tags for all students, teachers, and visitors that are worn EACH week to help any new person feel more at ease

_____Informal fellowship time before class when visitors are introduced in a nonthreatening environment (coffee or juice served as a courtesy)

_____Accurate records of all members and visitors including names, addresses, phone numbers, and so on

_____Responsible person to follow up with weekly phone calls on absentees and visitors

_____Someone to send out "welcome" letters to all visitors who come to the class

_____Designated persons who will provide transportation if visitors need rides to class

_____Persons responsible for "greeting" all students and visitors each week

_____Information in church bulletin or newsletter regarding weekly lesson topic

_____Information to neighborhood newspaper or local newspaper on special events or service projects

_____Creative bulletin boards in classroom; colorful posters or pictures on walls

_____Creative bulletin board outside of classroom with message inviting persons to come inside

_____Makeshift altar in classroom with open Bible displayed

_____Testimonies given by class members during church gathering, i.e., worship, fellowship dinners, picnics

_____An introduction of all guests each week during sharing time in class by greeters

_____Extra Bibles, hymnals, and curriculum so all members have copies as well as extras for visitors

_____Visitation team to go into neighborhood once a month to invite persons to Sunday school class

_____Monthly class socials where students bring visitors so they can get to know members personally

_____Ongoing class projects with invitations for visitors to assist (to give a sense of mission or purpose to the class)

_____Prepared lessons so visitors will feel compelled to return as learning takes place

_____Enthusiasm during the class time; a warm, cheerful class atmosphere to encourage visitors to come back

GROWTH FLOW CHART

STEP 1	**STEP 2**	**STEP 3**
Goals for Growth	Assignment to Member	Weekly Follow-through

Goals without assignment or follow-through cannot be realized.

PERSISTENCE IS THE KEY!

Sunday schools that are growing are usually the result of persistent leaders. Several years ago this persistence became a reality in action when Bob and I were assigned to a large church in the South. I volunteered as the youth Sunday school teacher, and the former teacher handed me the roll book with many names listed and said, "You really need to find out where these teens are. They certainly didn't come while I was teaching."

I was overwhelmed by the large list of inactives, but, quite honestly, I felt it was a challenge. "I'll find each one, don't you worry," I assured the teacher with enthusiasm. And slowly, I began visiting and phoning each teenager.

STEVEN, THE LOST SHEEP

I came to one inactive youth we'll call Steven. "Steven? Oh, just scratch his name off. We haven't heard from him in years," she said. *Does anyone even know where he is?* I wondered.

"Hello, Steven?" I questioned the young male voice on the telephone.

"Yes, this is Steven." No enthusiasm came from the receiver.

"This is your new Sunday school teacher," I said trying to be cheerful. "I'd like to invite you to Senior Highs this week. We meet at 9:30 in the education building."

"Church? This Sunday?" His unexcited tone expressed obvious doubt, and "we'll see" was all he said.

That wasn't so hard, I thought. I went to class on Sunday morning and knew that my room would be filled with enthusiastic and interested teenagers. But as I looked around the youth room, I knew Steven had not come. In fact, not many of the teens in the church had responded to my personal caring.

I'll not give up, I thought. And the next week I dropped notes in the mail to all the students and phoned Steven.

"Steven? It's Mrs. Bruce," I said with a chuckle. "Wanted to invite you to Sunday school again this week. Remember, the Seniors meet at 9:30."

"My Sunday school teacher again?" The teen seemed to moan as he spoke and acted a bit annoyed. But he ended again with, "We'll see."

Sunday morning came and again, no Steven. I felt like crossing the teen's name off the roll, but the Master Shepherd had other plans. Perhaps it was providential that our scripture lesson that morning was on the lost sheep. As I read the verse aloud to my class, I knew God was speaking to me:

"Jesus used this illustration: 'If you had a hundred sheep and one of them strayed away and was lost in the wilderness, wouldn't you leave the ninety-nine others to go and search for the lost one until you found it? And then you would joyfully carry it home on your shoulders. When you arrived you would call together your friends and neighbors to rejoice with you because your lost sheep was found'" (Luke 15:3-6 TLB).

The hundred sheep . . . were they the members on my roll? And the lost sheep . . . Steven? I had to keep finding the missing persons in my classroom, and, yes, Steven represented the one lost sheep. I was determined to find him. The persistence that now urged me on had become a divine nudge, a type of constant encouragement, and this persistence did not easily let go of the lost sheep.

Monday night, I made my regular phone calls to all members on the youth roster, and again sent out personal notes in the mail. The next Sunday was exciting as several inactive teens were in class, but still no Steven.

PERSISTENCE PAYS OFF

I called this young man for seven weeks. Perhaps some people would have given up by now. But I know God was behind me 100 percent as I made the weekly phone call again.

"Steven, it's Debbie again," I said in a singsong voice. Our conversations were beginning to take on a lighter note. We even got as far as talking about his new part-time job, his girl friend, and my favorite television shows.

"So, we'll see you on Sunday?" I asked hopefully after about five minutes. Again I received the same noncommittal, "We'll see."

Sunday morning came. My enthusiasm dwindled as I gathered my books and Bible for class. This job was starting to take its toll as I diligently tried to activate the stray members. Was it worth it? But as I walked into the classroom thirty minutes early and saw a lanky young man of about seventeen with a broad smile, I knew it was.

"Steven?" It had to be him.

"Yeah," the handsome teenager replied with a twinkle in his blue eyes. "Mrs. Bruce, I finally came so you would quit bugging me."

Bugging him? Is that what he thought? I know I blushed as I reacted to his comment, but the warmth I felt inside as I welcomed back one of God's precious children was memorable.

Steven came regularly to the Senior High class and even joined our youth choir later that month. One year later, Steven went on to college where he became a leader in the campus ministry.

Pushy? I don't think so. I would call it being lovingly persistent—not willing to give up so easily on God's lost sheep. Can't we all learn from the Master Shepherd who is persistent enough to keep searching for us?

HIGH RISK, HIGH RETURN

This persistence we talk about involves setting goals and following through with them and it entails a high risk on the part of your evangelism team. This risk of faith means a personal investment of time, energy, and prayers.

One Director of Christian Education in Mississippi told of an adult class in her church experiencing a substantial growth of eleven members within a six-month period as they established a CARE team.

"Our CARE team was made up of three members in the class," Patricia said. "This team worked with our pastor and me in sponsoring newcomers to the church. The team visited the newcomers, helped them get established in worship, and introduced them to key individuals on committees and groups. The result? Eight of our new members in the past six-month period are from this newcomer group."

Sponsoring newcomers is just one way to encourage growth in your Sunday school class. Working on inactive members or those "on the sideline" is another way. Inviting nonchurched people to attend class with current active members is another means of attracting new members to your class.

Where Do New Members Come From?

- Newcomers to the area and to the church
- Nonchurched persons currently in the community
- Inactive members in the church and class

Success is defined as "a favorable result, a good fortune." And Sunday school classes that are experiencing these successful results with numerical growth are motivated and nurtured by teachers who are persistent and who really care. The success of your growth plan depends on how seriously you address the personal needs of your present members, and on regular, constant prayer and communication with God.

How will you and your team proceed with membership growth? Remember, a high risk brings high return. Motivate your leaders to take this risk in faith as they

- **set goals for growth**
- **invite people to your class**
- **create a classroom environment that is appealing**
- **persistently use evangelism tools to seek new members**
- **affirm those present members in the Sunday school class**

4

Organize to Touch Lives

P|eople showing concern—that's a splendid definition for Sunday school teachers. Yet, as you are starting to realize, sometimes this is a difficult task as concern and class growth take time, energy, and can be emotionally draining.

Years ago, a few persons were concerned enough about young children to start what we now know as "Sunday school." In 1780 in Gloucester, England, a newspaperman named Robert Raikes was so concerned about local children being deprived of an education that he hired teachers to give educational and moral training on Sunday mornings.

There are people like Raikes who are still concerned about the Sunday school. And it is this initial concern that stimulates Sunday school classes to grow. But while wanting a Sunday school class to grow is admirable, unless action takes place, this growth cannot occur. It has been said that "we make a living by what we get out of life, but we make a life by what we give." *Growing classes are the result of concerned teachers who share God's love with others.*

First John 3:18 offers a challenge to all of us to begin a life-style of good intentions and deeds: "Little children, let us stop just *saying* we love people; let us *really* love them, and *show it* by our *actions*" (TLB). Let's look at some ways we can really love the persons who have interest in our class as we seek to evangelize those around us.

1. Organize for growth.

Having a growing Sunday school class takes time, and time is usually what busy teachers have little of. But if you organize for growth, you can keep track of important dates and events instead of waiting until after the fact.

Using a method as simple as a three-by-five-inch card file can help. On separate file cards, write pertinent information of class members and visitors. This wealth of information is the key to organized caring that doesn't take too much time. The following sample shows some of the key information to include on your cards.

STUDENT INFORMATION SHEET

Name: Elizabeth Ann Collins

Address/Zip Code: 3002 Pinehurst Rd., Apt. 211, City 22411

Phone: 388-2471

Birth Date: September 18, 1977

Parents' Names: Bill Collins and Ann Stevens (live with mother)

Address/Phone (if different): Bill Collins, 291 State St., City 22412 #282-3392

Comments:

(side 2)

Career or School: Junior/Jackson High

Personal Interests: Reading, Crew team, student government, movies, friends, youth choir

Visit 1: Date/comments/initials: Elizabeth is very interested in the Sunday school class and has several friends who are coming. Her parents are recently divorced, and she wanted to talk about this. Promised to come back next week (M.S.P.).

Visit 2: Date/comments/initials: After being regular in attendance for seven weeks, Elizabeth suddenly stopped coming. While visiting with her she mentioned that her mother was having surgery, and she needed to take care of her. Notified the pastor about this. Also called several youth parents to see if they would bring food for the family (M.S.P.).

Visit 3: Date/comments/initials: Checked on Elizabeth after her mother's surgery and all is well. Met her father for the first time. Elizabeth seems to be more settled considering the turmoil she has been through. Said she would be in class next week (M.S.P.).

On Sunday morning, check through the cards as you take class roll. Pull the cards of those students who are absent. Make cards for any visitors. Also pull the cards of any persons with birthdays or anniversaries. Perhaps one student is ill or undergoing personal problems—take this card out, too. Clip these cards together and take them home with you.

These cards are very valuable because they represent people that you must focus on in the next week either by a prayer, personal visit, letter, phone call, or other means of communication and concern.

2. Set aside a certain time each week that is "strictly for students."

We have found that after dinner on Saturday night is an important time to make phone calls to call class members. A teacher in a nearby church allows one afternoon a week to meet her elementary-age students for a soda or for home visitation. Another teacher takes one day out of her busy week to drive some elderly class members to doctor appointments or to the store. You might allow a period during the evening to talk with students on the phone or make a point to meet a student during the week. Talk about the person's interests—and listen! Find out what bothers them, what they dream about, and what they fear. Go further and read between the lines. Does the student appear to talk "big" but seem lonely and scared inside? Does he lack confidence in himself? These insights are important since they give clues to behavior and help you handle discipline problems that may occur on Sunday morning.

A middle school teacher tells of his success in meeting with students on their turf:

"I have permission to take the church van to a nearby middle school on Fridays during the school lunch break," he said enthusiastically. "The members of my Sunday school class gather their friends and pile into the van for a Brown Bag Bible study. We drive to the outskirts of the campus and picnic on the school lawn, then I lead a sharing group and Bible study. The response is tremendous. I am living my concern for them, and their commitment to Christ and to our class is the result."

3. Reaching out takes ACTION.

The Christian faith is an active faith! Using the cards you have pulled, write down ALL your good intentions to touch the lives of these special people, and keep this memo close at hand.

On our refrigerator we have an ongoing list with such "class notes."

Class Notes

____Call Susan after her mother's surgery on Tuesday.

____Take devotional book to Will.

____Write notes to students who were absent last week.

____Call the new family who just moved in.

As we complete each intention, we draw a line through the reminder and add more to the list. We take the cards that were pulled out on Sunday morning and stick these back into the file box for future use. This one list is readily available as our constant cue to follow through actively on those thoughts and priorities that are important.

4. Allow yourself to act on impulse as you show concern to class members.

When you feel a strong need to call a student or visit a class member, do it now! The longer you wait between the mere thought and the actual deed, the more likely you are to procrastinate and not follow through.

A professor we had in college challenged the students to act spontaneously in sharing feelings with someone.

"Say those special words 'I love you' out loud," he told us. "Call a friend with your voice, visit someone with your body, and hug a loved one with warm, caring arms."

"Take action," he preached to us the entire semester. "For only as you personally involve yourself in caring for others will your life be complete. It is through giving to others that you are rooted in the world."

To be "rooted in the world" by caring for others gives added meaning to our lives. While caring thoughts are a beginning, it is the action, putting feet to our Christian faith, that really touches lives and enables growth in the Sunday school.

5. Meet the needs of your class members and their families.

Stamping the lives of our students with Christ's model of ministry involves getting involved in the lives of others. To do this you must get to know the other person with the *agape* or selfless love that Jesus taught. This love works to understand the needs of others, then ministers in a personal way that will meet these needs.

When Jeremy's father was killed in a tragic car accident last year, his Sunday school teacher, Susan, was the first to meet Jeremy at his home.

"All I could think of was that my son, Trey, was in second grade like Jeremy," Susan said reflectively. "I kept asking myself how would I want Trey to be treated if this happened to him? What would I want people to say or do if this happened to my husband? I realized that the best I could do would be to go and sit with him and just be there. No words or actions were important except for Jeremy knowing that a friend cared."

6. Care enough to show empathy.

As you reach out in faith to those around you, don't shrug off the person's words and feelings. Rather, empathize with her.

While visiting in the third grade classroom one morning, we watched with interest as the Sunday school teacher talked with a parent. The parent was pouring her heart out about a subject that was obviously very dear to her. But, what impressed us the most was the teacher's compassion, sincerity, and empathy as she communicated her feelings of friendship and support. One could tell just from her expression that she really cared about what was being said.

A relationship that involves personal caring as you give of yourself to others means going that extra mile—together!

7. Value the healing power of touch.

Many in our society have been conditioned not to touch other people, but touch may be the key to positive self-esteem. A pat on the shoulder, a hug, or a loving back rub are often just as appreciated as saying the words "I love you." Often when words seem so meaningless, a caring touch can be the one action that communicates a living faith in God.

In a study at a large northwestern university several years ago, a number of young adults who checked out books at the library were given a handshake, a pat on the arm, or other touch by the staff librarians. After leaving the building, each student was questioned about the library. Of the students who had been touched, 100 percent reported positive feelings. But those who were not touched had either apathetic or negative feelings.

Using this nonverbal form of communication as you reach out and touch the lives of your students allows you to interact in a positive manner, especially when words aren't appropriate.

8. Prayer is important too.

C. C. Colton said, "We should pray with as much earnestness as those who expect everything from God; we should act with as much energy as those who expect everything from themselves."

Yes, prayer and actions go hand in hand. Be in constant prayer for your students—for actives, inactives, and visitors. Prayer can be a special communication you can use to let God know of your feelings and concern for all class members. And this special communication can be followed through with a card (it costs less than thirty cents for a caring letter) in the mail saying "you are in my thoughts."

Keep prayer lists with names of students and their loved ones who may be ill or going through personal trials, and act on these prayer lists daily as you lift their names up to God. Cross out answers to prayers as you see fit, and let the persons know they are in your thoughts.

Are you organizing to touch lives in your classroom? Are your members reacting positively?

People showing concern—that's what growing classes in the local church have in common.

5

Become an Inviting Sunday School Class

Our friend Sue was stunned when we asked her to serve on the adult class evangelism team. "Be on the CARE Team? I would rather serve refreshments."

Ron's reply was no more enthusiastic. "Call on inactive members? Invite people I don't know to Sunday school? Couldn't I just take roll each week or even teach once in awhile?"

All the publicity in the world will never guarantee class growth if there are not enough people willing to act as evangelists. Many people hesitate to make home visits or telephone calls for varied reasons—insecurity, lack of time, or just sheer apathy. Yet everyone has some type of faith story to tell. As class members are encouraged to take the risk of getting to know new, inactive, or shut-in members, caring takes place. And the Sunday school classes that are growing—spiritually and numerically—are usually the ones where outreach is taking place.

The members of one class were confronted with the need for outreach. "We realized that most of our church's new members are not transfers. Rather, these people come into the church on confessions of faith," said the class president. "And most of these people can get lost if they are not active in a specific class or group within the church. Realizing this, we formulated a plan to integrate these new Christians into the life of the church as well as nurture them in the Christian faith."

Another church experienced a similar situation. "Since we are in an older congregation, our rolls are filled with inactive members," one teacher explained. "When a new teacher comes in, he or she has no idea who these inactives are if they are not coming on Sunday morning. We had to devise a caring system where we could touch base with all the people—old and new—in our class."

Organization is the key to a successful "caring ministry" in your Sunday school class. In chapter 3, we mentioned how a specific team, the CARE team, can work with the teacher on following up on absentees, new members, and prospects for the class. Look how one teacher and her students worked together for class growth.

ACTIVE INVITATION

Mary Warner has been a Sunday school teacher for over thirty years. But more than telling you about the time she puts into preparation or into study, Mary loves to talk about being an "inviting" teacher with class growth as the result.

"Oh, yes. I do spend time studying my lesson each week, but, to me, seeing new people come into my class as they experience the love my students have to offer is just as important," Mary told us.

"My original group of students started with me years ago in the same classroom as today, in fact, we only began with a few regular members. I was determined to get the gospel message out to more so I began to seek new students.

"At first I visited the homes of church members I felt may have needed a class such as ours, then I started seeking out unchurched families in our neighborhood and asked students to bring these families to Sunday school," she continued. "After a time of actively inviting people to come to our class, I got some of my students to do home visits with me. Now the students do all of the phone calling and visits each week, and the exciting part of the story is that we are STILL inviting and still growing."

Teachers and leaders in the Sunday school today who give their classes growing reports agree with Mary as they talk about the joy of personally inviting and bringing students to the class on Sunday morning. These teachers affirm the necessity of meeting these visitors' needs with a warm, caring environment where God's grace can be received.

YOU HAVE A GIFT TO OFFER

As Christians, we are entrusted by God to preach the gospel to every creature (Mark 16:15). But before we can teach the message of the New Testament, we must reach out to our church and community and become "inviters" like teacher Mary Warner and her students. In the book of Acts we learn that God wants us to share the good news of the gospel message with every person who is not a Christian. We are commissioned to introduce that person to Jesus Christ and bring him or her into active fellowship with other Christians in Christ's church. What better fellowship in the local church is there than the intimacy found in a loving Sunday school class?

Your Sunday school class can be that special vessel where new persons are offered a greater purpose in life as they experience the gospel confrontation and thus, fulfill personal needs.

Maslow's theory points to several needs that are basic to every human personality. Among these are:

• The need to be loved
• The need to belong
• The need for self-worth

Knowing that people have these basic needs, your Sunday school classes can fulfill these and more. The men, women, and children in your church can invite and encourage new members to visit and join the ranks in their classes as they:

• Love each visitor
• Help new students feel ownership of the class
• Find potential in each visitor who comes through the door

40

A youth director at a recent Sunday school workshop told of her concern for lack of class growth. "I've motivated my members to invite other teens, yet once I get teens to visit my class, how can I get them to come back again?" Joanie asked. "I receive about five visitors a month in our class, but most never return. What steps do I need to take to get these kids involved?"

There are important steps Sunday school teachers and leaders can take to get visitors back each week. As a leader, you can teach your evangelism team ways to welcome visitors so they want to belong.

START WITH YOUR "CARE" TEAM

If you decide to begin using a CARE team in your Sunday school class, you will need to train these individuals to be effective. Perhaps these steps will help your class organize into a caring ministry. See chart on following page.

INFORM

Teach your CARE team that home visits are the KEY to continual church and class growth. Emphasize that caring is the key. Class visitors do not have to make a commitment to join during their visit, but rather students should attempt to begin building genuine, loving relationships with these newcomers.

In your information session, inform your CARE team that there will be times of rejection as well as times of acceptance. Knowing this ahead of their initial visits helps to affirm and give security to the volunteers.

INSTRUCT

"What do we say?"
"How long do we stay?"
"Must we pray after the visit?"

These are just a few of the questions that must be answered during your visitation training. Help your volunteers realize that each visit will be unique, just like the people they are visiting. Suggest taking along a copy of the class curriculum or a pamphlet about the church's activities to share with the person. Volunteers should stay just a few minutes on the first visit and remain sensitive to the people in the home. Train the CARE team to interpret the situation before they speak:

• Does the person seem uncomfortable?
• Have I interrupted a family time?
• Are body or facial expressions communicating special needs?
• Should I just listen during the visit?

As relationships are established, class visitors will be able to become more open with sharing their personal faith story and praying with people. (See questionnaire "An Examination of My Attitude for Witnessing" on page 44.)

Set up a file with addresses, directions to homes, and a special place for reactions by the visitors under each inactive and potential member's name. This filing system helps the teams become organized as visitation becomes regular.

Who to Invite to Class

- People we know well and have relationships with—family members, friends, neighbors, business acquaintances, and community workers; your boss or secretary, your physician, dentist, or beautician
- People who are like us—people who have similar values, interests, or socioeconomic levels as members in the class; people on community committees or in volunteer organizations
- People who would benefit from our class—a new family in the neighborhood, a recently widowed person, a single parent, someone going through a personal crisis, or anyone who is in need of care by others
- People who have access to transportation and can drive to the church—people who drive by your church daily and know its location
- People who do not have transportation—people class members will be responsible for each week by bringing them to Sunday school
- People who are searching to deepen their faith—new Christians, unchurched Christians, people who are looking for direction from God

List of People to Invite

List names, phone numbers, and addresses for CARE team use.

1. Family members: _____

_____

2. Unchurched friends: _____

_____

3. Friends/neighbors: _____

_____

4. Business acquaintances: _____

_____

5. Community workers: _____

_____

6. People who need support: _____

_____

7. People who need transportation: _____

_____

Instruct your CARE team to contact the minister or other church leader for additional help or a follow-up visit if there are problems that seem overwhelming.

INSPIRE

We have a commission to go out into the world, sharing our faith with those around us. Evangelism is mandatory to fulfill our duties as Christian disciples (Matt. 28:18-20). Paul wrote in Acts 26:13-23 that he was commissioned to go to the Gentiles and "open their eyes so that they may turn from darkness to light and from the power of Satan to God." How narrow our lives are if we feel too comfortable and secure in our Sunday school classes.

MORE WAYS TO CARE

Evangelism is not limited to home visits. The following suggestions represent other ways your CARE team can invite inactive persons to your Sunday school class:

Telephone: The telephone places a close second to personal visitation in reaching inactive members. Select someone who is talented in carrying on rich conversations. Keep the conversation brief, encouraging, and personal. Spend time listening while on the telephone; you may pick up indirect clues about why someone has not come to church. Avoid overreacting. Instead, be supportive. Always end with an invitation that is personal. Follow up from time to time once the person becomes more involved.

One class member said, "A few years ago, while serving on the CARE team of our class, I became aware of a young woman who came regularly to church yet never came to Sunday school. I telephoned the woman weekly, encouraging her to attend our class. We could never get together for a home visit because of conflict in work schedules. After a few months of constant phoning and sharing greetings at worship, a new face greeted me in our classroom. I was so excited to see her, we embraced with joy! She is now one of my dearest friends and is very active in our church."

Monthly Luncheon: A monthly luncheon at the teacher's home is a terrific idea for involving visitors and inactive people in the Sunday school class. Because the people get to know the teacher personally, they begin to take a greater interest in the class. What must teachers do?

- Risk being open and talk about your own life. This will free the guest to do the same.
- Be flexible with the luncheon. This could be a standard menu prepared by CARE team members or it could be a potluck lunch. Don't make it so organized that it becomes work instead of fun.
- Ask the guests for suggestions for the Sunday school class. Often when the members are relaxed and having fun, they may be more creative in their ideas.
- Make sure the guests are compatible with each other. If you have introverted, new persons coming, make sure you have outgoing, regular members of the class to carry the conversation, creating a welcoming environment.
- Share the love of the Lord, and commitment will be the result.

Cards, Letters, Bulletins: We've said it before, and we'll continue to emphasize this form of communication throughout the book. With a list of birthdays and anniversaries of class members, your CARE team can send cards and notes at the appropriate times. If an active member is out of town, a personal letter and church bulletin help convey a message of being missed. When a new person attends the class for the first time, send a personal note telling him about the class, the curriculum studied, and how much he or she is appreciated.

CARE team members should always notify the pastor when an inactive member or a prospect experiences a crisis. Often, if someone hasn't come for awhile, the minister loses touch with the person's needs. Yet, by depending on active Sunday school class members, your pastor can stay in touch with "who" is experiencing "what" in their life.

Once people experience the joys of serving on an outreach team, the CARE team, the enthusiasm increases. Most will agree that "it wasn't as bad as I thought." As lives are touched and inactive members come back into the fold, and new persons feel genuine concern, the CARE team can see the rewards of living the Christian faith as shepherds.

An Examination of My Attitude for Witnessing

| | | Not | |
Yes	No	Sure	
___	___	___	Am I a joyous Christian?
___	___	___	Do I look to the Holy Spirit in prayer, the Bible, and the church for guidance in my daily living?
___	___	___	Do my patterns of living reflect my basic Christian beliefs?
___	___	___	Am I willing to share out of my personal struggle and pilgrimage of faith?
___	___	___	Do I radiate confidence and assurance?
___	___	___	Will I become easily discouraged or angered by indifference or rebuffs?
___	___	___	Am I willing to share my faith in informal, natural settings?
___	___	___	Can I keep in confidence intimate thoughts shared with me?
___	___	___	Am I able to accept and appreciate Christian experiences and beliefs different from my own?
___	___	___	Am I able to support persons as children of God regardless of the condition in which I find them?

From *Visitation Evangelism, A Relational Ministry: Participant's Guide*. Nashville: Discipleship Resources, 1977 p. 14. Reproduced by permission of the publisher. As found in *Growing a Great Sunday School Class,* by Debra Fulghum Bruce and Robert G. Bruce, Jr. Copyright © 1994 by Abingdon Press.

6

Want to Grow? Start a New Class

In *The Pastor's Church Growth Handbook,* Richard Meyers tells of a group of ministers who participated in a research experiment. The ministers were divided into two groups. One group was told that if a Sunday school teacher resigned this year, do not replace him or her. Instead, these ministers were asked to combine the class with another and keep a watch on attendance for the year. The other group of pastors was asked to add another teacher and class to their present Sunday school program, reassigning the existing students to give all classes equal enrollment. They also monitored the class attendance during the year.

At the end of the year's time, which Sunday school program do you think had the highest enrollment and attendance? Believe it or not, attendance in the combined class had declined noticeably, resulting in loss in Sunday school attendance and church membership. But in the second group, all the classes that had divided had now grown back to the size of the original class. The result? These churches reported an increased total in their Sunday school attendance and in church membership (*The Pastor's Church Growth Handbook,* ed. Win Arn [Pasadena, Calif.: Church Growth Press, 1979]).

Yes, it is important to start new classes. More classes within your church mean more groups for more people. And more groups enable people to be a part of a close-knit Christian fellowship within the larger church, sort of a mini-church. But just how do you get started?

Some churches experience dissension when leaders suggest that a new class be formed. In one congregation, the pastor told of dealing with feelings of resentment when a new adult class was started because a few members of the other adult classes felt threatened by the enthusiasm. Yet, the wounds healed quickly as the new members extended God's love to more people.

No matter when or why you decide to begin a new class, the project must be well planned to be successful. The following steps outline an effective procedure in planning a new class.

1. Recruit a core group.

To build on the strength of your present Sunday school classes, this group of leaders should include members from a present class, along with other adults (or youth) who have expressed interest in the new class. This small group will serve as the backbone of the new class. By combining the present leaders with new leaders on the committee, you will be able to have wisdom and experience along with energy and new ideas to work with.

The first goal for your core group is to establish the need for an upcoming class. Questions that must be answered are:

- WHO needs the class?
- WHERE will the class meet?
- WHICH age group will be attracted?
- WHAT are the concerns and issues of that particular age group?
- WHEN will we begin the new class?
- WHO will teach the new class?
- HOW will we promote this class?

Once you are able to speak specifically to a particular group's needs, the core group can most effectively recommend teachers and curriculum.

In starting a new class, we find it best to have a certain curriculum or book of the Bible chosen for the group to study rather than have these new members make this choice in the first meeting. Our reasoning is that the topic chosen is a real drawing card to the new members. In considering curriculum for the "New Class," ask the following questions:

- What denominational material and curriculum are presently available?
- What are the specific needs and interests of the group you are trying to recruit for the class?
- What curriculum and Bible study material have been recently used by other classes?
- What is the total cost of the curriculum, special workbooks, or other resources?

The core group also must set goals for the new class. Not only should you project attendance and membership goals as you plan for your new Sunday school class, but you should also prepare a list of benefits.

The last planning step your core group should take is to select a kickoff date and time. Make sure this does not conflict with the church calendar. Launch out in faith!

2. Plan an active publicity campaign.

The publicity crusade for a new class must be carefully planned and implemented. For a new Sunday school class in one church, the head of the steering committee told of printing brochures listing the course of study along with some personal quotations from other active members on "Why I Go to Sunday School." These brochures were handed out in church and mailed to inactive church members. Lists of names of persons in the specific age group were obtained and phone calls were made. A director of Christian Education at another church told of his steering committee making home visits as they personally invited new members to join the class. This was followed by providing transportation for some of the new members to the first meeting.

46

Obtaining the support of your pastor is vital in publicizing the new class, as he or she has many contacts during the week. The pastor is also a key resource person for suggesting innovative lesson ideas. You may want to ask the pastor to teach some of the sessions of the new class, since he or she will be known to most prospective class members.

Ask your pastor for a few minutes during a morning worship service to tell parishioners about the "New Class." Many lives can be touched as people give personal witness to the importance of the Sunday school program. (See chapter 7 for more promotional ideas.)

3. Allow for fellowship.

The morning of the new class, be sure to allow ample fellowship time. Serve coffee and doughnuts to encourage those late sleepers to arrive on time, and name tags are a necessity.

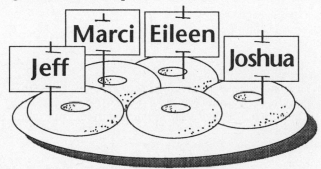

Again, invite the pastor to participate in this opening session. Make sure the teacher has adequate time to guide the Scripture study and encourage participation during the first meeting.

4. Ask for response.

Ask for response from various class members after the first session. Did the lessons meet the needs of those in attendance? Did the members seem comfortable in the classroom setting? Follow through with phone calls, home visits, and more letters to newcomers for a few weeks after the initial meeting until a Sunday school habit is formed.

5. Discover, develop, and use new talents.

As new members come into the class, gently guide them into leadership positions according to their spiritual gifts and talents. They will feel ownership of the class as they become the "inviters" and recruit more members for the group. Newcomers to the church, especially new Christians, have the greatest potential for evangelism as their friends and acquaintances may also be unchurched persons or other new Christians. It will not be long before you witness how a small group can grow as more Christians are challenged to reach out and serve.

6. Exercise prayer and patience.

Sometimes, after following all the proper steps of planning, the class still gets off to a slow start. And, while we should constantly be aware of quality in our classes, quantity does not hurt! The Koinonia class we belonged to went for months with the same four initial couples. Yet, these members stuck together, and slowly more adults came and joined the fellowship. The class grew so much that new young adult classes were formed. We learned what can happen through the power of prayer along with much patience.

Do you want your Sunday school attendance to increase? Perhaps now is the time to reach out and involve more adults in your Sunday school program by beginning a new class.

Promotional Letter for New Class

Use the following form letter to style your own promotion for the new class. This letter is for community members who are not associated with the church today. You can adjust the letter according to the specific needs (current church member, age of student, and so on). The important factors include a personalized mailing that answers these questions:

- **Who** is the class for?
- **Where** will it be held?
- **When** will it meet?
- **What** will the class study?
- **How** can the person get to the class?

Date _____

Dear _____:

Welcome to _____ church! We are excited about having you as part of our church family.

On Sunday, _____, we will start a new Sunday school class just for _____ (children, youth, singles, young adults, middle adults, mature adults, Bible study, or other focus). The new class will meet in the _____ building in room _____. While we usually will meet at 9:45 A.M., on _____, we will meet at 9:30 A.M. to share in fellowship time. A light breakfast and coffee will be served (or doughnuts and orange juice for youth).

We have chosen to begin a study of _____ as we get started in this new class, and remind all members to bring their Bibles.

If you have any questions or need transportation to the class, won't you call me at _____? I'd be happy to answer any questions or help you in any way so that you can be there with us. (If applicable: A nursery will be provided during the fellowship time, then children will go to their respective classes.)

_____(name of person), we look forward to having you with us on the _____ (date).

Faithfully,

Teacher's name

7

Publicity Does Pay Off

For many years, the Committee on Religion in American Life (RIAL) has worked diligently to keep people aware of the importance of religion in the life of our nation. How did RIAL share its news? Using television and radio, as well as print media (newspapers, magazines, brochures, and so on) the committee worked with the Advertising Council to get its message across.

Obviously, publicity is an effective and necessary means of communication.

So what about publicizing the Sunday school? Have you ever wondered if MORE people would be MORE involved in your Sunday school class if they had MORE information about it? Maybe the adult class has ministered to the same twenty people for years. What about those youth in your congregation who do not attend a class? Could your children's attendance pick up if people knew more about the curriculum and activities? Perhaps a publicity campaign would be that special tool for sharing the message of your class with those in the church and community.

The Great Commission challenges, "Go into all the world and proclaim the good news to the whole creation" (Mark 16:15). An active publicity campaign, using various media, accepts this challenge to reach believers and nonbelievers.

Promotion is an effective tool for sharing how God is working in your Sunday school class. Before you determine what type of publicity you want to use for your Sunday school class, consider the following questions and answers.

1. Who are you trying to reach?

Know your audience. Identify the age group, interest area, and other pertinent factors before you begin your publicity. Narrowing down the field is vital to create a message that will appeal to your audience.

2. What do you want to say?

Keep your message simple, but include important dates, times, and places of the events. Gear the general tone to the average person, and stick to your main points. "Piggybacking" upcoming events only confuses the reader; those letters usually wind up in the trash can.

3. How are you going to say it?

A catchy title or slogan captures immediate interest. In class publicity, we have used themes such as, "Give Five, Come Alive!" or, "Operation Faith Lift" during recent attendance crusades. For a brochure or card telling of an upcoming event, a simple rhyme or creative logo may help emphasize the facts. Again, keep the publicity simple, visually attractive, and to the point. Save explanations for later.

4. What media do you wish to use?

There are many different ways to publicize Sunday school classes. Some classes diversify with several different methods, while others zero in on the one they find most successful.

Examine the most popular methods of publicity that various groups use. Then select a method that appeals to you, and get busy!

NEWSLETTERS/BULLETINS

The broad audience and ease of distribution make this method extremely attractive. Whether handed out to members of a surrounding community, mailed to a certain zip code area, or mailed just to the members of your class, the message gets out.

A newsletter or bulletin should greet the reader personally and answer the reader's question, "How can this help me?" Include a name and phone number for added information after each article or invitation. Be creative, and the possibilities for your publication can come alive!

For a children's event, you might enclose a colorful balloon with the date and time of the event written on it. Include instructions to inflate the balloon for more information. Invitations can also be printed on a small slip of paper and inserted in the balloon with instructions to inflate and pop the balloon to get the message.

For another event, one might print the announcements on a brown paper bag and title it, "YOUR YOUTH CLASS IS IN THE BAG AT CENTRAL CHURCH." Be innovative and spark excitement in your audience.

Pieces of a large puzzle can be sent to adult class members with the instruction to bring that piece in on Sunday morning. "We are all parts of Christ's body" the message can read as you encourage persons to attend on Sunday morning and celebrate their oneness as a group of Christians.

BULLETIN BOARDS

Bulletin boards should be centrally located in your classroom or right outside the door so visitors and members can see them. Appoint someone to be responsible for regularly updating the bulletin boards and keeping them visually attractive.

Themes are attractive and eye-catching. Cartoon characters, seasons, holidays, or even a "play on words" make excellent themes. Be sure to keep the bulletin board uncluttered and colorful. Pictures featuring various class members in action help to portray an active program.

The main danger of bulletin boards is that they readily become outdated or bulletin "bored." There is nothing more drab than a faded announcement. Keep it fresh!

FILMS/SLIDE PROGRAM

Use family gatherings to publicize your Sunday school class with a film or slide program. Ask a photographer to take pictures of the class during group activities. Pictures help to communicate what a Sunday school class is and what it does.

PERSONAL TESTIMONY

Ask your pastor for a few minutes during a morning worship service to report what is going on in your Sunday school class. Include people of all ages in this personal sharing, and let them tell of the activities they experience weekly. Many lives can be touched as people give personal witness to the importance of the Sunday school class.

DRAMA

Skits, clowns, and puppets can be used creatively to grab the attention of inactive young people. They can be used to enhance an announcement during worship, between classes, at a social time, or any all-church gathering. Communicate that your class is alive and interest will grow.

ONE-ON-ONE SHARING

There is no publicity quite like personally inviting someone to class. Each active member should be encouraged to invite people to your program. Telling what the class is all about and bringing the people if necessary will demonstrate the value of the Sunday school class. As this caring takes place between the members, the true meaning of Christian fellowship is experienced.

Remember—make your class publicity ATTRACTIVE, make it ACCESSIBLE, and show people in ACTION. The Sunday school is a vital part of the total ministry of your local church. Where else can people of all ages join a caring, supportive community, learn how to change their lives, and hear God's Word taught by experienced and caring leaders? With added enthusiasm shown through an exciting publicity campaign, your Sunday school class can begin to fulfill Christ's challenge to "Go into all the world!"

Publicity Tips to Try Today

1. Start a class newsletter.

The Discovery Class in our church has a monthly newsletter that the president does on his personal home computer. In this newsletter, members and visitors are told of upcoming speakers and lesson topics, particulars on the monthly social, class prayer concerns, and anything else that is pertinent. A fourth and fifth grade teacher in another church tells of sending a one-page newsletter each month to her students. In this mailing, she lists all visitors to the class, upcoming birthdays, and notable achievements the students have made at school and in the community. According to this teacher, "The kids feel special and keep coming back each Sunday!"

2. Send a class bulletin home each week with students.

Information can include a welcome to the visitors of the class, an overview of the day's lesson, information on upcoming parties or social events, and phone numbers members can call for transportation to class.

3. Make a creative bulletin board outside your class door.

Does your class stand out? It can if you take time to create an innovative bulletin board right outside your class door. Use vibrant colors and catchy titles to get the attention of those who walk by. You want others to say, "This class certainly enjoys being together!" Include on your board a listing of prayer concerns, the topics of the month's lessons, and other pertinent information that may encourage visitors to come in.

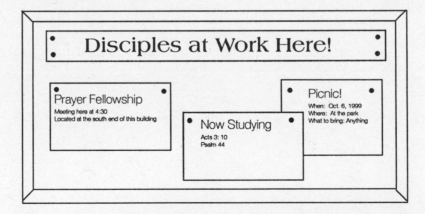

4. Take a video of your class in action and show this video at a family night dinner.

A youth or children's class could do a role play or drama using dialogue from the curriculum. An adult class could do a personal testimony of "What Sunday School Means to Me." Think of how your class could "promote" the benefits of the class to others and capture this on film.

5. Make a commitment to tell unchurched friends and family members about the Sunday school class.

Growth becomes realistic if each member can bring or invite a member. Most people attend church because *someone invited them* to come.

Try these additional ideas for promoting your class:
• Announcements written on paper to hand out to class members
• Church bulletin
• Notes taped on students' clothing for younger students to get parents' attention
• Personal letters mailed to parents and families
• Phone calls prior to the event
• A phone chain with class members calling several people each
• Posters in the classroom, church, and neighborhood advertising the event
• Public service announcements to local radio and television stations
• Press releases to local newspapers, followed up with a personal phone call

Sample Press Release

In preparing news for the press—television, radio, newspaper—the questions WHO? WHAT? WHY? WHEN? WHERE? HOW? must be addressed. Other tips to remember include:
• Type your media release on church stationery, if available.
• ALWAYS have a contact person and phone number on this page.
• Keep the release to one page, typed and double-spaced.
• A picture is invaluable. If you can, always include a photograph of people in action and attach the names of featured persons.
• Follow up on this release with a phone call several days later to see if more information is needed.

Church name and address: (preferably church letterhead)

_____

Date: _____

Contact: Your name _____

Phone: _____

FOR IMMEDIATE RELEASE

First Church Hosts Easter Egg Hunt

All Westside children between the ages of three to ten are invited to an Easter Egg Hunt sponsored by the youth of First Church. This annual event is free to the public and will be held on Saturday morning, April 2, from 10:00 to 12:00 on the church lawn located at 300 Main Street. Interested children are asked to bring a bag or basket for gathering eggs. Those who want can also bring two canned goods for the homeless ministry.

For more information or transportation needs, please call Mrs. Martin at 000-0000.

Did the release answer the important questions?

- WHO: For all children in Westside ages three to ten
- WHAT: An Easter Egg Hunt
- WHY: To be a good neighbor and to collect canned goods for the homeless
- WHEN: Saturday morning, April 2, from 10:00 to 12:00
- WHERE: The lawn at First Church at 300 Main Street
- HOW: Call Mrs. Martin for more information or transportation

If you want to make sure your release is picked up by the media, remember to keep your event:

Relevant: It is important to the community as a whole.
Creative: No one else is doing anything like this right now.
Timely: It is a first to meet this particular need.

8

Creativity: A Must in the Classroom

So you've checked your attitude, your CARE team has started their duties, and visitors are coming to class. Now what?

Author and educator Judy Gattis Smith challenges teachers to bring their creative best to the task of teaching. "Some people think creativity is a talent or personality trait, but creativity is not a special gift. It is a normal and necessary part of everyone's thinking," Smith writes. "You are creative because you are unique. There is no one else in all the world just like you. At its core, teaching is a creative act. No one will teach a class in just the way you teach it because the lesson is filtered through your unique life and experiences. Teaching at your creative best will excite and interest students so much that they will keep coming back for more" (Judy Gattis Smith, *77 Ways to Energize Your Sunday School Class* [Nashville: Abingdon Press, 1991], p. 11).

Creativity is at the very heart of Sunday school growth. You can have scores of visitors to your class, but without innovative teaching, these interested persons may not stay. The teacher who uses creative flair in inviting students to class, in involving these students in the lesson, and in creating a classroom environment where God's love and grace can be shared, is the very teacher who will experience growth—quantitative and qualitative.

There are many ways teachers can be creative in the classroom; methods too numerous to discuss in this book! But some key creative tools we will focus on include using:

Teamwork,
Props
and
Creative Discussion

WORKING IN TEAMS HELPS STUDENTS BE CREATIVE

"Sunday school is over already? We just got started on this report."

"Can't we go a few more minutes? Our team wants to talk about this question a bit more."

"Will we get to continue this banner next week? I have a super idea for displaying the Christian symbols."

Does this sound like your Sunday school class? These students are working in teams as they get involved in the class lesson and are proving that learning is taking place. Perhaps no one fully understands how learning takes place, but we do know student involvement is a major factor. When the material taught is absorbed, and the students can personally relate to it and then act upon it, learning has taken place.

Learning occurs when a change has taken place. We have new insights, new ideas, new goals. "Learning takes place when the following changes occur: (1) addition of information, (2) increase in understanding, (3) acceptance of new attitudes, (4) acquisition of new appreciation, and (5) doing something with what has been learned." (Adapted from Malcolm Knowles, *Informal Adult Education* [New York: Association Press, 1950], pp. 30-31.)

For every action the teacher takes, the class member will display a reaction in any group situation. Let's see how this works out in a typical Sunday school setting.

1. Creativity encourages learning.

Two Sunday school teachers, Mr. Winger and Ms. Sutton, use the same curriculum each Sunday morning. Both teachers average fifteen students in class each week; both tell of preparing for several hours for the Sunday lesson. Mr. Winger and Ms. Sutton have standard size classrooms with chairs for students and several tables lined up against the wall. But that is where the similarities end.

In Mr. Winger's class, the students are virtually uninvolved in the class lesson. "We sit quietly and try to listen to what Mr. Winger teaches," one student said. "He is an excellent Bible scholar, but somehow we are missing the point. We can't get involved in the material."

Hank, another student in Mr. Winger's class, commented, "There are always two or three people in the class who do all the discussing at the end of the lesson. The rest of us sit and wait for the dismissal bell because we don't feel a part of this discussion."

On the other hand, if you were to look in on Ms. Sutton's class, you would find small clusters of chairs throughout the room, people roaming around the class library table searching for information, and even a group of several adults working on a banner for the class.

According to students in this class, Ms. Sutton is a creative teacher. "It's not that she is teaching every minute, but she guides us in finding the answers to our questions. We are able to discuss the lesson some of the time with her, but after she gives the information from the curriculum, we are free to go and dig deeper with the resources she provides."

Melinda, a young woman in Ms. Sutton's class, commented, "I like the way we get in teams of three or four to discuss the questions she gives regarding the lesson. I am very shy, and this helps me to feel comfortable enough to speak out and give my opinion without feeling intimidated."

The difference in teaching style can often mean the difference between students learning or not learning. Ms. Sutton has found that in order for real learning to take place, class members must creatively absorb the given material and be able to relate it to their lives. On the other

56

hand, Mr. Winger prefers to use the large group setup that offers fewer possibilities for interaction by class members. In fact, when a group exceeds fifteen persons, the number of persons who can participate in a discussion is limited. Large groups are usually dominated by a few aggressive individuals while everyone else sits and listens.

The learning process begins with the known. In fact, before you can teach effectively, you must consider what knowledge your students already possess. Language development, experiences, previous teachings, maturity level, and social awareness all combine in every individual. But how can you know all of these factors about each student? Are there effective teaching methods that can help you encourage learning?

2. Small groups are important.

Small group interaction using teamwork is the most likely place for individual interaction to take place. When students work as small teams, you can simplify teaching material to meet each student's needs. Students have a chance to discuss the given material, relate it to their lives, ask questions, and come to conclusions that may enhance learning.

A student team may be two or three members in a small class or ten to fourteen members in a large class. But many teachers avoid teaming students for good reasons. Small groups require more time for the teacher as more members will be involved in communicating. The teacher must constantly oversee the individual groups to make certain they stay on the topic at hand. Working in small groups as a team is often risky. Teams can go off in totally unexpected directions, but it is the enthusiasm of this exploration that enables students to begin learning in a way that relates to their lives.

There are numerous types of small groups that can be used in the Sunday school classroom.

- **Buzz Groups:** for sharing opinions and reporting; talking about feelings; relating to the story
- **Small Group Discussion:** pooling information; exploring how a person in the story or verse feels; reaching conclusions
- **Creative Dramatics:** role playing; presenting pantomime; using puppets; clowning; plays
- **Project Groups:** working on a service project for missions
- **Research:** reading and reporting; compiling information; keeping journals
- **Craft Construction:** making murals, mobiles, scrapbooks, banners, collages
- **Drawing or Painting:** expressing feelings through art or design; making timelines; interpretive dance
- **Creative Writing:** writing prayers, paraphrases, songs, poems, prose, news articles, short stories

When you choose to teach in teams, the following guidelines are necessary to ensure a response.

State the goal clearly. Tell your students what you expect them to do in their teams. If you are specific with the intended goal, your students will know what to aim for.

Outline the process for the small group. Do not leave it up to your students to figure out how to reach the goal. If you are asking for the teams to do research, offer suggestions on how to find the material. Say, "Try looking up the information in the Bible commentaries on the library table." Or, "Perhaps you might go to the pastor's office and interview him on this question." The more specific you are in showing the way, the better outcome your students will have.

Oversee the group. Walk around the room and listen in while the teams are in progress. Of course, you must allow the different teams to set their own pace. Yet if one team seems to be struggling with the topic or more interested in a topic of their own, such as the Friday night basketball game, you must intervene and offer suggestions for finding answers and reaching the stated goals.

Encourage evaluation. Tell the teams to evaluate their results before entering back into the class group. Did they find the desired answer? Did they meet the stated goal? Was each member allowed to speak and be an active part of the small group?

Allow for sharing. Often, one of the biggest stumbling blocks in using small groups is that teachers fail to bring the groups together for sharing. The final step, that of personal sharing, is the most important step in small group interaction. While the members have opened up to each other in the small groups, it is only when the students pool their information in the large group that you can be sure learning has taken place.

Affirm and encourage. While the various teams interact in group sharing, the teacher needs to affirm the participants' responses. The rule "all is OK" stands here to encourage all members to speak their opinions. Comments made as the different members speak, such as "very interesting" or "I like that idea" are necessary. This builds up the individuals in the teams and provides strength to the total group.

PROPS ADD EMPHASIS TO THE LESSON

In most cases, the students in your class will respond to your lesson content *if* the teacher has creatively involved them with the material. Teamwork is an excellent tool to encourage creative learning; another way to do this is by using teaching aids or props.

A teaching prop is an audio or visual aid. A prop can be as simple as manila paper and markers, modeling clay, wire for sculpturing, old magazines for making collages, or scraps of fabric and burlap for making banners. It can be as extensive as a slide show set to music, a special recording for background effect, or a poster covered with magazine illustrations to stimulate discussion. Props can be used with other teaching methods such as buzz groups, role playing, or research teams to enhance the material being taught.

Teaching props can also be used to provide information on historical moments. Often a short, contemporary film on a specific liturgical season such as Christmas or Easter speaks more effectively than an hour of lecture. While some information may be disseminated through books, leaflets, or pamphlets, students tend to respond when they are actively involved with their five senses while the information is being received. Charts, maps, and posters can show distance, time, or other relevant factors. Information given in this way is more likely to be absorbed because it does affect the student's senses, and he or she becomes involved. Teachers regularly use props such as biblical costumes, background music, voice tapes, and so on, to add intrigue and excitement to the lesson, resulting in added classroom interest.

1. Teaching aids capture attention.

Displaying a poster or playing a game also assists in capturing the attention of your classroom audience. Often many students are intimidated when it comes to sharing their thoughts or feelings in class. Using a game can allow the class members to "play" while learning the material presented in the Sunday school lesson. Popular board games such as the Ungame can enable students to discuss feelings while they are having fun during a Sunday school lesson on the Christian's response to living in the world today. Other games such as Bible Scrabble or even Bible computer games can be used with great success in the classroom.

2. Teaching aids bring the subject to life.

Teaching props can also help to bring the subject to life. After discussing the topic of aging, one fifth grade class gave little response. "Then we used several suggestions in the lesson for helping the youth 'feel' what aging was like," the teacher said. "One way was to stretch rubber bands across their hands to simulate the effects of arthritis. Another way was to try to read the lesson quarterly through thick glass that made the letters blurry. Our young people were able to get involved with the subject. The students responded, and some attitudes toward aging were changed," the teacher reported.

3. Teaching aids help students express feelings.

Another Sunday school teacher tells of regularly using props as simple as plain paper and markers to give his students an opportunity to create and draw their feelings concerning the lesson. After a series of lessons in one class on the Crucifixion and Resurrection, the teacher gave the students pieces of thin wire to bend into sculptures representing their feelings. One young person chose to depict the Crucifixion and made a shape of the cross. Another chose to create an abstract design of his feelings regarding Jesus' untimely death. Then another young student chose to model the Resurrection out of the wire and sculpted a large butterfly.

All students were able to talk more freely about their feelings as they held the creative sculptures in their hands. The props had allowed the young people a chance to express their feelings with a hands-on tool while they interacted with their fellow students. Students could also use clay to mold figures representing their feelings, markers and paper to draw their feelings, or paint to create abstract and creative designs.

4. Carefully select teaching aids.

If you choose to use props for Sunday school lessons, make sure they are well chosen, and can supply the facts, information, and background material to meet the goals of the Sunday school lesson.

Choose props according to group's ability, interest, and experience. Are members of your class musical? Artistic? Dramatic? Some students may respond to lyrics in contemporary or Christian recordings. Others prefer slide shows, pictures, or visual aids. Still others would choose hands-on objects, collections, or displays. By knowing the individual interests of your class members, you can create props that speak to and interest the majority of students each week.

Consider the uniqueness of each individual in your class, the level of maturity, and the personal knowledge about the lesson subject. Primaries would accept a film on the Christian's response to aging differently from early teens. A display of biblical artifacts would have a different meaning for an immature eight-year-old than for a mature fifteen-year-old.

Choose props to complement the lesson. Clay modeling, wire sculpturing, and painting are excellent examples of ways to involve class members in the lesson. But they will not lend themselves to every subject. These props are best used when feelings must be expressed. Often if the lesson is about a new land in the Bible or a new group of people, pictures of these places make appropriate props. Illustrations of biblical geography and culture can be found in picture-book versions of the Bible story, in the lesson quarterly, or in magazines such as *National Geographic.* As students see what they are hearing, they are more likely to process this information internally. Maps enter into the classroom picture as students find the biblical town on a world map. Let the students travel across the map back to their hometown, and ask appropriate questions about the trip.

Change teaching aids often to prevent boredom. Filmstrips are excellent, but should not be used each week. A plan that allows for continued interest might be to use filmstrips one week, a hands-on experience like sculpturing the next week, songs and music the third week, and a costumed speaker the fourth. This will keep the class members stimulated each week without creating boredom. As your students look forward with anticipation to the next week, learning can take place.

Select props with attention to available time. A film will not be as valuable if you have little time left for discussion or questions. A good rule of thumb is to allow fifteen minutes for an introduction or presentation, at most thirty minutes for the film, and then another fifteen minutes for a discussion of the high points of the film.

CREATIVE STORAGE

Keep material for props in your classroom. A prop shelf should have the following:

- markers
- paper
- tape
- modeling clay
- scissors
- wire for sculpturing
- tape recorder and blank tapes
- video camera and blank tapes
- chalk
- glue
- scraps of fabric
- burlap for making banners
- old magazines
- biblical pictures or photographs
- maps

CREATIVE DISCUSSIONS HELP TO BREAK DOWN BARRIERS

Classroom discussions offer another break from the typical lecture-style class. But while having a discussion with students in the Sunday school about a specific topic, idea, or Scripture verse can be trying, even for the most creative teachers, an active discussion of a Bible verse or an idea from the curriculum can be a tremendous experience for both teacher and student. Feelings can be revealed, new insight will be gained, and personal growth can take place as communication occurs.

Let the following ten tips offer insight on leading an active discussion in your class.

1. Know your students.

Find out their faith history, their personal hang-ups, their struggles, their dreams and goals. Ask questions about their personal likes and dislikes, and listen! Be perceptive as you establish new friendships and caring relationships with each class member.

2. Know the age group you are teaching.

Read books that describe specific developmental traits. Talk with other teachers in the church who have insight into the specific age and observe the unique qualities of the students in your class.

One teacher explained that she asked the children what some signs of God's love were. A preschooler answered, "A stop sign and an exit sign." The word *sign* had a completely different meaning for the adult and the child. Thoughts and feelings will come alive if you use vocabulary that is age-appropriate and that children can relate to.

3. Know your material.

Preparation for a stimulating and creative discussion also involves knowing the material. Read your lesson until you feel secure with teaching it. Reach out in prayer and Bible study as you search for answers to the suggested questions in the material. Ask your pastor or other Bible students for additional information, if necessary, so you will be well versed in the subject.

4. Prepare questions that relate to your students.

Once you feel comfortable with your material and students, prepare discussion questions that not only relate to the material presented, but that also relate to your class members. As the class members begin to trust you, relationships will begin to form. Soon the students in your class will be experiencing a closeness where thoughts can be expressed, barriers lifted, and new ideas generated.

5. Write discussion questions that are specific.

In writing questions for discussion, be specific with your choice of words. Often the question may need to be paraphrased if the class is unable to relate to it. Be sure to do this in your "homework" time, not during class time.

Prepare questions that are open-ended, which call for expressing feelings, ideas, and creative thoughts. Avoid using questions that require a simple yes or no answer.

Discussion Starters

If you want to challenge students to a rousing class discussion, use questions that are open-ended rather than questions that require a yes or no answer.

RIGHT	WRONG
What would you do in this situation? (open)	Has this ever happened to you? (yes or no)
Why do you think she would do that to her friend? (open)	Have you ever done that to a friend? (yes or no)
How could she change the way others viewed her? (open)	Could she change the opinion of her friend? (yes or no)
Can you think of some Scriptures that can help us learn about God's love? (open)	Does the Scripture in 1 Corinthians 13:13 tell us about God's love? (yes or no)

6. Let the person speaking have his or her opinion.

Accept what each person has to say during discussion time, and thank the students. Some students, even adults, will express a simple theology that is unlike yours. Yet the person's thoughts are important in a classroom discussion, and you hold the key to his or her self-esteem and further development in the faith. Each student's confidence in the classroom depends on your approval.

If you feel you must challenge or correct a student during discussion, do so as you teach, not in contrast to what has been said. A friend said, "I never spoke during Sunday school after my seventh grade teacher told me that my ideas were wrong. I didn't ever want to be wrong again."

7. Affirm and encourage the students.

Discussions are most beneficial if the teacher constantly affirms the participants' responses. Encourage all members to speak their opinion. Comments made as the different members speak, such as "very interesting" or "I like that idea" are necessary. This builds up the individual and provides strength to the total group.

Refrain from being critical, even if the idea is totally irrelevant. Rather, use each statement and build from it. Comments such as, "That may be true; can anyone else add another thought?" or "That may be one way of looking at it, but how does it apply to the Scripture we are studying?" help to rescue the discussion from becoming trapped. This also saves the speaker from unnecessary embarrassment.

One teacher told of how to avoid having one student monopolize the discussion in her large class. "There is always one person in my youth class who wants to talk the entire time," José said. "This is not to say that the discussion is not interesting, but everyone needs a chance to express their opinion."

"I have found that one way of avoiding a takeover in the discussion by one student is to say, 'We haven't heard from Susan yet,' or 'James, let's listen to what Paul has to say right now.'"

While there may not be an exact manner of discouraging one person from controlling the class discussion, the teacher needs to be in tune with the class personalities and find a polite way of setting time limits.

8. Use discussion props, if necessary.

Often students respond more readily if you have a teaching aid or prop to stimulate discussion. Follow the guidelines in this chapter as you creatively add props to your classroom discussions.

Our early elementary teacher keeps a complete set of teaching aids in the storage closet. In this closet, members have brought in old magazines, current event articles filed by topic, biblical pictures from old curriculum, maps showing places around the world, and other odds and ends. The contents of this closet provide assistance to the teacher on numerous occasions as she seeks added ways to bring the message to life.

9. Listen and react.

Observe the participants in the discussion. Watch for body language that may be telling the opposite of what the member is verbalizing. For example, if someone is relating feelings of peacefulness and security, yet is nervously sitting on the chair twitching and shaking, he might be crying out for personal caring. Again, this is where the teacher has the responsibility to affirm, to uplift, and to encourage the individual.

Watch each member as he or she speaks. Use direct eye contact, even if you begin to find your mind wandering. Your interest in each speaker adds to the affirmation.

10. Share your personal faith in God.

Is there a lull in the conversation? Has the discussion reached a peak but not a conclusion? Now is the time to bring the message of the Gospels. Have Scripture ready to communicate with the class relating to the discussion topic. Tell of your own encounters with God through Jesus Christ. Relate these discussion topics to your personal faith-story, and be prepared to lead members to a saving knowledge of your Lord. By sharing your own ups and downs your class can grow as Christians, and you can grow as a faithful disciple.

"Sharing my faith is what I look forward to each Sunday morning as I teach," Charlene said. "I look for appropriate moments during the discussion to interject moments of my past when God spoke to me and made a difference in my life. These special times during the discussion seem to bring the topic to reality as the students see that someone they know really did have a conversion experience. As I share of moments when my life was touched by God's hand, my students interpret the Scriptures as being real for their lives."

Remember, learning takes place when a person becomes totally involved with the material being presented. As your class rolls begin to fill with new members, creatively involve these students in active learning as you use props, innovative discussions, and work as teams in the classroom.

9

Meeting the Needs of Your People

Why can't things be the way they used to be?" a frustrated Christian educator said at a recent church growth seminar. "Remember when Sunday was the day everything was closed except for the church? Now we have to deal with adults who must work on Sundays, and therefore, children who cannot attend at this time. What can we do to increase our classes?"

Another teacher questioned: "I have two classes of students. Because of divorce and step-families, most of my students come every other week to class. Are there some ways I can meet the needs of these children?"

Many churches are finding that to grow, they must meet the needs of their people. And in some communities, people are more available during weekdays than they are on Sunday morning. Classes that were once limited in attendance by members' work schedules, week-end travel commitments, or just poor planning, are now thriving as they change their format to meet the needs of the students.

INNOVATIVE SUNDAY SCHOOL CLASSES

The following ideas represent some innovative Sunday school sessions that can meet varying needs in your community.

1. Something on Saturday "S.O.S."

A northwestern congregation tells of having a "Saturday School" for children and youth who cannot attend on Sunday morning. This two-hour class combines Bible study, crafts, singing, and recreation and meets the life needs of thirty-four youth who normally wouldn't be involved in the church. According to the pastor, the approach to S.O.S. is very similar to vacation Bible school.

"We plan fast-moving activities, easy crafts that can be taken home that morning, and have different members who don't teach Sunday school as the leaders," he said. "The exciting result of this alternative Sunday school is that some of the families are now coming to worship the next day and bringing the children to the regular classes."

Children who meet on Saturday can greatly benefit from Bible-based lessons such as those in *Pathways to Discovery,* published by The United Methodist Publishing House. Other resources include current Sunday school curriculum or vacation Bible school resources.

2. Sunday Breakfast Club

Another church tells of an alternative adult class that meets at 7:00 A.M. on Sunday morning.

"We've had tremendous success with our breakfast club class for singles," Maria, the leader, said. "These are people who work late shifts on Saturday night or many work on Sunday at local malls. We meet in the social hall, and different members take turns preparing breakfast. After a quick breakfast, prayer time, and Bible study, we feel rejuvenated to go into the world and be Christian disciples."

3. Wonderful Wednesdays

Many churches across the globe tell of having Wonderful Wednesdays as a complement to the Sunday school program. This group of children and youth meets Wednesdays after school for a choir program, Bible study, and recreation. Many of these children never attend church on Sunday morning because of parents' varying schedules, but are able to hear the Word of God midweek.

4. Home Study Groups

Some Sunday school classes meet during evening hours midweek in the members' homes as they minister to those who cannot attend at the traditional time. These home studies thrive on the personal touch they are able to give to outsiders who normally would not come to church.

5. The Kitchen Class

Perhaps space is the greatest stumbling block for class growth in your congregation. It doesn't have to be a limitation at all! Many churches take advantage of the most remote places to have Sunday school, including such classes as the Kitchen Class, the Parlor Class, the Library Class, and the Outdoor Class. Look around your facility for a space that is quiet and, preferably, covered from the weather. If you don't have four walls, use mobiles to hang up decorative pictures. A standing chalkboard can be used for teaching and is portable. Chairs can be brought in, set up for class, then folded and stored during the week. Let your imagination take over as you think of the possibilities for ministry in your Sunday school.

HOW TO START AN ALTERNATIVE CLASS

When starting a new class that meets at a nontraditional time, planning is crucial. As a teacher, you need to consider the following steps to ensure its success:

Sun	Mon	Tues	Wed	Thur	Fri	Sat
Kitchen Class			*Wonderful Wednesday*			*S.O.S*

1. Select a meeting time, place, room, and date.

Place the information permanently on the church calendar, keeping the lines of communication open with the staff.

2. Select a leader(s).

Ask someone familiar with the education program in the church to assist in getting the program off the ground. This person does not have to lead the Bible study or teach the curriculum, but needs to lead the group once they have convened.

3. Know your audience.

Identify the target age group, specific concerns or interests, and other pertinent factors before you begin your publicity for the alternative class. Narrowing down the field is vital to start a group that will have specific appeal.

4. Publicize it effectively.

Keep your message simple, but include important dates, times, and places of the events. Gear the general tone to the specific audience you are trying to reach, and stick to your main points.

A catchy title or slogan captures immediate interest. In publicity for a Singles Breakfast Club, members told of using the theme "Give Five, Come Alive!" and encouraged participants to try the group for a total of five Sundays. For a brochure or card telling of an upcoming group meeting, a simple rhyme or creative logo may help emphasize the facts. Again, keep the publicity simple, visually attractive, and to the point. Save explanations for group meetings.

There are many ways to promote your alternative class as discussed in chapter 7.

5. Don't limit the number involved.

If you find you planned on ten children and twenty show up, be sure you have a backup team ready to assist. If you have more interested members, don't turn them away! Start another group.

6. Involve the pastor.

Encourage him or her to visit the support group as needed. Ask the pastor to invite community members in the group to visit the Sunday services or other groups.

7. Communicate with the congregation.

It is important that the regular members of the church know about your alternative classes. Keep information going to members in your church bulletins or newsletters, and try to involve as many members as possible in the leadership of the class.

8. Encourage participants in the alternative class to attend worship.

Once you have established a strong class, begin encouraging these members to get involved in the total life of the church through worship, committees, and other traditional classes.

Alternative classes are just one innovative way leaders in the local church can reach out to affirm members and nonmembers alike as they meet the needs of a changing society. These classes can help some congregations experience Sunday school growth who otherwise might not.

A GROUP FOR J.O.Y.

How can teachers work together to form an alternative class? One congregation found a group for mature adults called the J.O.Y. group (Just Older Youth) to be successful after some strategic planning.

The steering committee prepared a survey that was distributed throughout the congregation and later to the surrounding community. This survey asked questions pertaining to age, job status, and the person's interest in a Sunday school class for older citizens that would offer Bible teaching, education, recreation, and fellowship within the local church.

The steering committee began to evaluate various Christian study materials and chose issues and questions of importance to older persons. Some of the topics selected were :

• dealing with declining health
• living on a fixed income
• wills
• retirement years
• understanding Social Security and Medicaid
• recreation

With an initial enrollment of twenty-three adults, leaders were chosen to launch the group. The weekday program was planned to begin with a musical activity, hymn sing, and handbell workshop for those more musically inclined. Other activities during the morning session included simple exercises, isometrics, and other icebreakers. A film, speaker, or minister's study were scheduled to follow this. After the planned program, the group varied the lunch hour with bag lunches, potluck lunches, and eating out.

Once the J.O.Y. weekday program became stable in membership, the group began to get involved in service, volunteering at church, or having a group outing to various recreational and historical sites around the area.

After a time of meeting and growing, this nucleus of older adults began going into the Sunday school classes at church. Other older adults who could not come to the biweekly program time, celebrated with their friends as they studied the Bible together on Sunday morning.

Reportedly, the congregation began to notice their older members more as the J.O.Y. members became active in all areas of the church. One of the young adult classes, many of whom were miles away from parents and grandparents, began an Adopt-a-Grandparent program, taking under wing those members of the J.O.Y. class who did not have relatives nearby. Children were able to be loved and cuddled by the older members as the people became more active in the weekly suppers and studies. And as one might expect, this helped the members of the J.O.Y. group to feel important and needed.

10

Reaching Out with Fun and Fellowship

T he Bible is filled with stories of how Jesus and the people "broke bread together." Dinners on the grounds or potluck suppers are the mainstay of many churches as members join in fellowship to share a common meal. Some educators feel that one of the main characteristics of a meaningful class is class members eating together several times during the year. This may be the monthly social event, it may be an occasional covered dish or carry-in dinner, it may be picnics or other outings, or it may be only coffee and rolls every Sunday before class convenes. Not infrequently it is a combination of several of these (Lyle E. Schaller, ed., *The Parish Paper* [Yokefellow Institute, March 1974]).

Most people—children, teens, and adults alike—want to be known, to belong to a group, to have fellowship, to have fun. Persons usually think of a Sunday school class in terms of its educational role with the church, but it can also fulfill an important need as a fellowship group in the church.

In our church, the strongest Sunday school classes are those who have regular monthly outings or parties. Our fourth and fifth grade class celebrates with after-school parties and a hayride with caroling at Christmastime. Another adult class meets monthly for a theme dinner or potluck supper. Another class varies their outings from a luncheon out after church on Sunday to a barbecue at someone's home to a special dessert party for class members (See excerpts from the article "Making Time for Class Fellowship" by Debra Fulghum Bruce [*Adult Bible Studies* Teacher Helps/Summer 1993]. Copyright © 1993 Cokesbury, Nashville, TN).

No matter when these members join, the message is the same: we care about one another and want to share our Christian friendship together.

FELLOWSHIP OPPORTUNITIES

The opportunities for fellowship within a vital Sunday school class are endless! Class members can spend time together outside the church, getting to know one another through picnics, retreats, sharing groups, parties, and more. The following are proven ideas used by classes of all ages:

SEASONAL ACTIVITIES. Holidays provide a regular excuse for celebration and fun. Christmas caroling, a Thanksgiving hayride, a St. Patrick's Day progressive dinner, or a Valentine's Day candlelight dinner are just a few ideas.

Whatever the occasion, have a theme. It adds to the festivity and helps build enthusiasm toward the outing. Be creative within your theme.

GAMES. Games can be used within a class lesson or outside class time to bring students together. You can teach a new skill, enjoy an old skill, or simply have fun playing together in a noncompetitive way. Some classes have "game night" where members bring favorite board games to someone's home and enjoy the fellowship of class members.

RETREATS. Go off for the weekend—with children or without. Throughout the nation are many camps and retreat places. Check on the availability of camps in your conference or state. Often in getting away for a few days, people are able to relax, to get to know one another better, to affirm others, and to be affirmed. Camp-outs, seminars with outside speakers, family weekends, marriage enrichment themes, or district or conference sponsored retreats offer these possibilities.

SERVICE. In the local church, as well as in the outside world, are many opportunities to serve. Helping at workdays at church, volunteering to baby-sit in the nursery, or mowing lawns for the shut-ins of the church are needs that exist in every local church. Other projects include giving parties at retirement homes, writing letters for the invalids at nursing homes, preparing and taking food to persons in need, adopting a grandparent, and working to earn money to buy equipment for the church or for a church mission project.

SHARING GROUPS. Small groups stemming from the Sunday school class can provide an additional setting for personal growth. Meeting informally yet regularly, for sharing and enrichment or for a Bible or other type of study, class members grow in their understanding and in their caring for one another.

SPORTS. Softball teams, volleyball games, and basketball tournaments are forms of active recreation for all ages in the Sunday school. Sports events are especially helpful for those occasional class members who aren't ready to commit to every Sunday morning, but who still want to enjoy class fellowship.

PLANNING HINTS

Planning for your class fellowship times is just as important as planning for your class study times. The following are some helpful hints.

1. **Choose persons to handle the details, such as where and when the party or project will be, and so forth.**

This committee should also be responsible for getting publicity to members two weeks before the activity. They may need to make phone calls the week before the event to wrap up last-minute arrangements.

2. Plan regular opportunities for fellowship.

Many groups have found that with monthly socials, outings, or service projects, attendance rose during class time. Persons began to like one another because they got to know one another, which is often hard to do in a church school classroom on Sunday morning.

3. Invite and bring new persons to the fellowship times.

Reach out to unchurched persons in the community. They may feel more comfortable coming into your group first at a social than being a guest on Sunday morning.

4. Remember to include persons who for some reason cannot attend the class on Sunday morning.

They may be teaching in the children's or youth division, or their jobs may require weekend or nighttime hours. The monthly social allows them to still feel a part of an active Christian group.

5. Use this fellowship time to get to know members who seem reserved during class time.

Usually, people will open up in a relaxed, small group whereas they may feel more intimidated in the classroom.

6. Use fellowship opportunities to reverse the downward slide in your attendance this year.

The following ideas on the annual growth calendar represent ways you can use fellowship opportunities as you motivate students each month to take action and enjoy your class.

Annual Growth Calendar

January: Focus on Epiphany. Plan a special three kings celebration for your class that focuses on the giving of gifts, and invite all Sunday school classes to join you. Fliers can go out to all members asking for gifts of canned goods to take to area homeless shelters.

February: Focus on love and caring. Around Valentine's Day, have a class candlelight potluck dinner. Children can bring parents as their "loved ones" to the dinner or adult class members can bring spouses or a special friend. Use this time to encourage inactive members to take part in the fellowship of your class as adults provide transportation. Publicity can be in the church newsletter, a special red and white heart-shaped invitation, and personal phone calls.

March: Focus on prayer. March can be a special time for class members to get together to pray for growth. A prayer vigil can be held each Saturday morning, then members can go into the neighborhoods visiting those inactive members on the roll. Send letters in the mail telling church members of your prayer concerns and ask for support from other classes as you seek to grow.

April: Focus on the Resurrection story. Easter is the celebration of new life! Children can invite friends and neighbors to a class-sponsored Easter Egg Hunt on the church grounds. Youth and adult classes can be sponsors of this for community children. Publicity should be extensive, including radio public service announcements, press releases to area newspapers, direct mail fliers, and so on.

May: Focus on the Holy Spirit. Pentecost can be understood by all ages. Join with other Sunday school classes for an assembly and talk about the "church universal." Using red as the color theme for publicity, encourage everyone to wear red on this Sunday and decorate the classroom with red balloons and white doves.

June: Focus on outreach. If you are holding your vacation Bible school during June, follow up on all children who register with a personal home visit. Make sure that these children are aware of your Sunday school class, and let parents know that you can find transportation, if necessary, to bring them to Sunday school. Remember, parents will need a class too! Adult and youth teachers will need to get copies of the vacation Bible school roster and make phone calls or personal visits inviting these new people to the classes.

July: Focus on freedom. Independence Day offers a time to appreciate the freedom we have in our country and the freedom we have as Christians. A special picnic on the grounds for your class can be publicized in many ways. Print your invitations on a brown bag or even write on a red-checked fabric. Remember, creative mailings are a perfect way to get anyone's attention and to let others know that your class is alive and active.

August: Focus on camp meeting. Change your class format for August as you hold Sunday school camp meeting. Send out personal notes to all interested members and inactives, announce your camp meeting in worship, and invite other classes to attend. Start your class time with singing of the old hymns and use this time for members to share memories of how Sunday school has touched their lives. Encourage members to dress informally during this month as the temperatures soar. Also during August, begin telling members and inactives of the upcoming Promotion Sunday with special mailings and phone calls.

September: Focus on education. Back to school time reminds all of us of the need to stay involved in education. As you promote new members to your class, be sure you have taken time for a home visit with the families. Adult teachers need to make sure home visits have been made and that all students have copies of the curriculum, whether they attend the class or not. This is a perfect time to update that class bulletin board and display new class rosters on the wall. Try starting an annual tradition by taking a class picture this month and framing this for future generations.

October: Focus on fall. As the leaves change and the temperatures begin to drop, teachers are given the perfect opportunity to have fellowship dinners and parties. A hayride on a cool October evening, a fall festival party complete with bobbing for apples, or a potluck dinner one Sunday evening can keep the interest going in your class. One class focuses on service to others in October with the annual Rake 'n Run. All members meet at the church with their favorite yard rake, then they proceed to the homes of shut-ins. The members rake each yard and bag the leaves as quickly as they can, then "run" to the next home. Not only does this project provide a great benefit for the shut-ins, it gives the class some creative fellowship time.

November: Focus on giving thanks. Thanksgiving receives the spotlight this month for most Sunday school classes as they plan outings or fellowship dinners. You can encourage class members to spend time writing "thank-you notes" to those who have touched their lives. You can also thank members and inactives for some special way they have touched your life. As you develop a personal relationship with each member, they are more likely to respond to your call for class participation and attendance.

December: Focus on the Christ child. December affords the Sunday school teacher the perfect opportunity to reach out and touch new lives for Christ. Inactives generally feel that gentle nudge to attend church this month, and you can take advantage of their presence by making your classroom experience one of joy, learning, and celebration. Plan on fellowship times before the class meeting and bring doughnuts, orange juice, and coffee for the members. Let your students be in service this month as you give Christmas to those in need. And share Christmas with those who cannot come to church as you go caroling. Include class members in making cards for inactive students or friends who are not attending any Sunday school class.

Sunday school growth is not just an emphasis that occurs once a year. Classes that are experiencing growth tell of ongoing activities and opportunities for fellowship all year long. As you make plans each month to reverse the downward slide in your class attendance, you will see the benefit of increased attendance and changed lives for Jesus Christ.

ENJOYING FELLOWSHIP WHILE GIVING TO OTHERS

Service projects in your Sunday school class can provide more time for fellowship and building group spirit as students work toward a common goal of helping others. The teacher has the responsibility of making sure that the project is suited for the class and will help spiritual growth occur. Fulfilling this responsibility requires careful planning and implementation. Perhaps the following suggestions can guide your plans for a class project.

Talk with all members before making ANY service commitments. Have a discussion period with the group and write down their ideas on a chalkboard or a large piece of manila paper. In this brainstorming session, let them know the "sky is the limit" so students don't feel intimidated about their thoughts on service. While you are brainstorming ideas, take a survey of talents your class members have. Try to answer the following questions during this survey.

SERVICE PROJECT—TALENT SURVEY

What are the group's strengths?

_____

What are its weaknesses?

_____

Will the entire class make a commitment to participate? (Write down the names of those who will commit here and if it is a children's class, be sure to check with the parents involved to confirm this commitment.)

_____

_____

_____

Do the members want a short-term or long-term project?

_____

After you have isolated the talents and limitations of your class members, discuss the needs in your local church, in the community, and in the world. Tell children the list of needs and write these here.

Local church needs:

_____

_____

Community needs:

_____

_____

World needs:

_____

_____

Which category do your class members' talents fit best?

_____

_____

An older elementary school class may choose a nursing home as an ongoing project. They can provide the patients with seasonal decorations. Or class members may decide to write letters for those who are unable to do so or to sing as a group to provide entertainment for the residents. Present a list of suggested service ideas to the staff members of the nursing home so they can guide you to the greatest needs.

A youth class may decide to paint their Sunday school room to raise money for a missionary, or to visit church members who are confined to their home. Discuss these projects and any others you have in mind with your pastor and with members of the appropriate committees in your church. These people will be able to provide helpful suggestions and support for the undertaking.

Projects in the local church could include maintenance and repair of the church building for older youth, spring cleaning, nursery work during special services, ushering as a class, office work, yard chores, and upkeep of the parsonage.

Service to others in the church could include visiting shut-ins with younger elementary school children, doing yard work for persons with handicapping conditions, baby-sitting for youth classes, and providing transportation to church or to a physician's office for older youth.

Service to the community could include involving the parents of your Sunday school class members as they work as a team in assisting with social service agencies in raising funds, running errands for older adults, serving with the Meals on Wheels program, providing day care for children, and collecting clothes and furniture for people in need.

Help for people beyond the community could include mission trips to Third World countries, raising funds for mission workers, and collecting clothes, food, and medical supplies for disaster victims.

In helping your class members select a service project, avoid becoming overzealous. Committing more time than the children, youth, and adults can give may create feelings of failure in the class members and disappointment for those the class is helping. Start small with your project and grow as you help the class members recruit volunteers from the class and church.

Christian service springs from personal love and concern. Be sure the project your class members select is based on such love and concern.

HELP CLASS MEMBERS SET REASONABLE GOALS

After your class members have selected a service project and have made sure it is right for their age and skills, help them set goals for the venture by asking the following questions:

• What are we trying to accomplish with this project?
• Who will be in charge? (A strong leader is important.)
• Who will participate on the day of the project? (Have names and phone numbers available.)
• When will the project take place? (List dates and times.)
• What is the completion date? (Always have an ending for evaluation.)
• What factors may hinder the project's success? (weather, other church or community activities, school hours, funding)
• What factors will benefit the project? (timeliness, adequate funding, willingness of volunteers)

Involve as many of your class members as possible in the project. Other church members can also be involved and may have the skills that could be used in carrying out the project.

For example, some people might offer financial assistance or help drive to the project. Others could offer spiritual support through prayer. Encourage all class members to become involved so that no one will feel left out when the spiritual rewards of serving others are shared on Sunday mornings.

If your class members choose a project outside the area, be sure to publicize the venture throughout the church and community. Some possible methods include press releases to the local paper or church newsletter, a bulletin board with maps showing where the project will take place, or a slide show using a family night supper to get the entire congregation excited about the project. Local television and radio stations generally have a community service announcement time you could use to advertise your venture without cost.

Take advantage of all tools available to promote your project. The more publicity you have regarding the undertaking, the more enthusiasm the class members will create among those around them. People will see your class members "putting their feet to faith" as they describe their activity.

ALLOW AMPLE TIME FOR REFLECTION

Periodically reflect on what is taking place during the service project. Are class members actively involved? Are the members able to share God's love with those around them? Reflection helps the class members understand that the Christian life involves taking care of others. You may want to refer to *Beyond Leaf Raking: Learning to Serve and Serving to Learn* by Peter Benson and Eugene Roehlkepartain (Abingdon Press, 1993) for additional ideas for integrating learning and service.

EVALUATE POSITIVELY AND GROW!

As the teacher, lead the students in your class in an evaluation session following the completion of the service project. Ask:

• Did the project work out as planned?
• Did all class members participate fully?
• What could have made the project go smoother?

Evaluation is vital to understanding the process necessary for ministry. However, remind your students that the evaluations should be positive and directed toward the project rather than negative and critical of people.

Keep a folder or notebook listing the steps involved in carrying out the venture. Refer to this list as other projects are suggested.

PUTTING FEET TO FAITH

Service projects can give Sunday school classes excellent opportunities to join hands to help those in need. Helping the underprivileged in the community, raising funds for disaster victims in the United States, or building schoolhouses in the wastelands of a far-off country are all examples of Christianity in action.

"Putting feet to faith" involves caring for those around you—even for those you do not know. Service to others also fills a strong need for class members as they feel a sense of ownership in the class.

11

Winning Tips from Winning Teachers

Is Sunday school growth becoming a reality to you and your members? As visitors become regulars in your Sunday school class, you may experience some stumbling blocks that you didn't expect. Whereas you previously knew the members on roll and were able to minister to them effectively, having more persons on roll and establishing new relationships is not always easy.

As we discussed in chapter 2, enthusiasm is vital for ministry in the Sunday school classroom. An enthusiastic teacher conveys genuine caring and concern from the heart. This teacher also incorporates creative ways of reaching out to class members and encourages them to care for others.

In this section, we've invited some enthusiastic and "winning" teachers from around the country to share ideas of how they "grow" a class.

PRAYER PARTNERS

In the classes I lead, I like to take a snapshot of each member in the class. On the bottom of each photo we place a label with the person's name, address, and phone number.

Each week we shuffle the photos like cards in a deck and distribute them to the class members. The photo you receive is the person you are to pray for during that week. The class is encouraged to use the phone number or address to call or write the person a quick note letting them know they are being remembered in prayer that week.

As new members come into the class, we take their photos as well and add them to the "deck." We also share prayer concerns after distributing the photos so that people might know how to pray specifically for the person in the picture they hold in their hands.

Sometimes a person in the class gets their own photo. We ask them to keep this and to concentrate on praying personal prayers for themselves that week.

Matthew Hartsfield
Pastor and Teacher

SET GOALS, COMMUNICATE, AND CHALLENGE MEMBERS!

A Sunday school class needs clearly defined goals. In our case, we met with the outgoing officers and solicited their opinions (and thereby their support), and sent out a questionnaire to all class members, asking them what they wanted to see/hear/do/learn in the coming year.

Communication is also paramount! In today's age of the personal computer, it is a snap to create a "class data file," and then use this for form letters, flyers, mailing labels, and so on. Personal computers can also chart attendance and allow you to send mailings selectively to those missing class for a number of weeks. If you don't have a computer, ask for assistance from your church office as you do frequent mailings to members.

Mobilize! If a class is lethargic, get 'em moving with some easily accomplished projects. In our class, we embarked on a simple renovation of our classroom and built a tremendous amount of support and camaraderie in the process. When presented with the need for a Homeless Breakfast, the members rose to the challenge, and a new and enthusiastic group of volunteers took over the project.

Solicit questions—the harder, the better! Deep and provocative questions may have to be answered by the pastor, but what wonderful growth and discussion ensue in the process. The answer to all of life's questions are in the Bible, and a sincere pursuit of answers can be Sunday school's greatest gift to its participants.

Sunday school needs to be fun. Our class was so inhibited that we got our own coffee pot and started to provide doughnuts (fresh and warm) each week. Now we have to be reminded to keep our door closed as our social period at the beginning of class disturbs our neighbors. Still, it is easier to tone down a happy class than to motivate a somber, sleepy one.

Dave Hastings
Adult Class Teacher

STAY ON TOP OF YOUR NURSERIES

We have found it important to stay on top of our nursery situation to keep attendance in all classes. Parents today want excellent nursery facilities for their young children. This means keeping the nursery rooms spotless, disinfecting the toys each week, changing the linens, having a sign-in sheet at the door, and especially having nursery workers parents know and trust.

When our church started taking care of our nurseries, young adults responded by being regular in attendance and bringing their older children to Sunday school.

Hariette Woodall
Young Adult Teacher

CREATIVE CLASSES CAN INVOLVE ALL MEMBERS

It is my belief that every member of the church family, regardless of age or stage in life, should be considered a candidate for a possible Sunday school class. With that in mind, we decided to try an innovative way of involving older adults in the Sunday school. Over ten years ago, we started a telephone Sunday school class known as "Listen in His Name."

At the moment, there are twenty-eight persons involved, and I am their teacher. We use our denomination's curriculum and during seasons such as Advent and Lent, the special seasonal studies are used. Participants at home do not have copies of the curriculum. Because of their varying states of health, their ability to juggle a telephone and curriculum is often difficult for them.

As with all conference calls, everyone can hear the other participants as well as the teacher and can respond accordingly. It is an exhilarating experience! The class has developed into a caring community. Many times when someone has a need or is in the hospital, the operator will inform me and we will be able to respond quickly. We celebrate birthdays, anniversaries, and other significant dates. Each class session is closed with a prayer for each member of that class.

The operation of the class is done by way of a preset conference call arrangement with the telephone company. Around 9:00 A.M., the conference call operators, usually out of Atlanta, contact each member of the class, and they are put on hold. At 9:15 A.M., when all the class members have been contacted, the phone company calls me in the office. We have roll call and proceed with the lesson. We are in operation from 9:15 to 9:45 every Sunday morning. Percentage for attendance is quite high, usually in the 90 to 100 percent range. Some members have been part of this venture since its inception; others have joined along the way. The point of recruitment is usually through contacts that I have in visitation with older adults or from other adult class members. When we began the class there was a limit to the number that could be absorbed on the telephone bridge of twenty-four, but as you can tell, we have exceeded that now and there is virtually no limit. Technology has improved to the point where that is no longer a consideration.

The members of this class are visited not only by me as a staff member but also by our CARE committee. This is a type of Sunday school class that any church, regardless of size, could develop.

Paul Juvinall
Minister of Visitation and Adult Ministries

TEACH CREATIVELY AND KEEP THE ATTENTION OF THE CLASS

As a teacher of elementary grades, I know it is important to have ongoing class participation each week. I have found that children look forward to the creative props and teaching helps with the lesson each week, and this has helped our attendance tremendously.

Board games are especially fun for our class—from games that come with the curriculum to homemade games relating to the lesson. One favorite for my fourth and fifth graders is based on the television game "The Wheel of Fortune." We divide into two groups and use a "wheel" from a game purchased at a local store. The children spin the wheel and guess consonants, buy vowels, and try to solve the mystery puzzle—usually our Bible verse for the day! The group that solves the puzzle gets to pick prizes from a special box.

One Sunday during the Lenten season, we made unleavened bread. The children did all the mixing, cutting, and frying. We served the bread with jelly and apple cider. The children still talk about Passover and their class Seder meal.

Creative activities help stimulate children to be regular in attendance as they wonder, "What are we going to do today?"

Diane E. Bond
Elementary Teacher

TAKE ADVANTAGE OF PERSONAL COMPUTERS

Use the personal computer in your Sunday school classroom. One way is to present the Scripture by way of the computer monitor using one of the new *Bible for Windows* software or use CD-ROM technology and view the Scripture on a large television screen. You can devise a multi-media program for students to use individually or as a group with on-screen Bible questions.

With young adults, using the computer as a teaching aid makes great sense. The computer is part of their life-style at home and at work, while adding to the interest of the classroom discussion.

Mike Dishman
Young Adult Teacher

TEACHERS MUST BE INVOLVED IN THE TOTAL CHURCH

I have found it mandatory that teachers stay involved in the total church as dedicated Christians. How can a teacher lead children or adults when the students never see their teacher attending worship on Sunday morning?

Vergie Smith
Evangelism Chairperson

KEEP RELATIONSHIPS ONGOING WITH THE PARENTS

Our team of teachers visits the parents of newborns in our congregation when new births are announced. As parents of young children, we tell them the importance of church and Sunday school attendance for the Christian family. We also provide these parents with some parenting pamphlets, a certificate, and information about our nursery.

It may take awhile before the parent brings the child to Sunday school and nursery, but we believe in starting a relationship with the family when the children are very young and continuing this with added visits, phone calls, and cards in the mail.

Samantha McCall
Nursery Coordinator

ALWAYS WEAR A SMILE AND LISTEN!

The teacher's attitude on Sunday morning will set the tone for the class. I have found it important to give at least ten minutes before the lesson begins for my students to "air" their problems—school, peers, family concerns. The teacher must really listen and try to hear what the student is trying to say.

There have been many Sundays where my lesson plans changed dramatically when students seemed to have other concerns on their heart. The teacher must remain flexible as she gives time to meet the needs of the students.

Eva S. Vaughan
Junior High Teacher

ENCOURAGE CLASS PARTICIPATION: FOCUS ON SPIRITUAL GIFTS

After trying for weeks to get our young adult class off the ground, we did a study on spiritual gifts. We wrote each gift on the blackboard and had class members call out their names if they thought they had that particular gift. Now, we had a list! This one list gave ownership to the students; they felt they were important and had a special God-given talent to share.

After making the list, we decided as a group that the teachers would "teach," the administrators would "lead," the hospitality types would hold the "socials," the helpers would "feed the sick," and so on. This enabled us to break down the classroom responsibilities so that many would take part instead of just one person leading many. It has also helped us in establishing prayer chains, calling those who are ill or absent, having regular class socials, and having prepared teachers each week. We have realized the biblical truth that we are all parts of one body. Working together, we are able to be far more than we would be alone.

Our class believes in the absolute power of God in guiding us as a group of Christians and in bringing new persons into the fold. Our teaching team believes in edification of each member, and our goal is to let members see how God's Word relates to our lives today. We also provide a tape ministry with recordings of each class lesson. Members and other interested persons can check these tapes out of the church office each week.

We have a monthly newsletter that gives class news, an update on our missions, dates of socials, lists of those who have been sick, and so on. We also include a list of visitors taken from the visitor's sign-in book in this direct mail piece.

Diann Catlin
Young Adult Teacher

DON'T FORGET WHO YOU ARE TEACHING

This one tip has helped me for years: REMEMBER, YOU ARE TEACHING A PERSON . . . NOT A LESSON.

Sunday school teachers must stay focused on the individuals in the classroom!

Margaret McDougle
College Teacher

83

Winning Worksheet

What area do you need to work on in order for your teaching ministry to radiate enthusiasm to those around you? Look at the following categories (low, average, high). Are you a winning teacher?

	LOW	AVG.	HIGH
1. My knowledge of the Bible			
2. My understanding of the curriculum I teach			
3. My knowledge of the age group I teach			
4. My attitude for teaching each week			
5. My involvement with the students outside class time			
6. My ability to motivate students to invite friends and unchurched persons to class			
7. My confidence in sharing my faith in Jesus Christ with my students			
8. My involvement in the total church program			
9. My personal prayer time outside class			
10. My ability to set reasonable goals and work to meet them			
11. My compassion for students who are difficult or having problems			
12. My concern for those who need transportation or special invitations to bring them each Sunday			
13. My ability to get assistance when I feel overworked			
14. My time spent in preparation and personal caring each week			
15. My use of creative resources and teaching helps to add to the lesson content each week			

If your enthusiasm remains high on most of these criteria for a nurturing teacher, you are well on your way to a winning ministry! Find the areas you need to work on, and prayerfully set personal and class goals to become an enthusiastic winning teacher.

From *Growing a Great Sunday School Class*, by Debra Fulghum Bruce and Robert G. Bruce, Jr. Copyright © 1994 by Abingdon Press.

12

Our Challenge as Christians to Teach the Gospel

Believe it or not, even though many denominations are on the decline with membership, some leaders in the local church still feel that growth is not important. Some say that pastors and leaders who want to grow numerically do so merely to build their own egos. This may be the opinion of some, but in our ministry and in the ministry of many, Sunday school growth is important for a variety of reasons. A growing class helps individuals as persons make a dedication of their faith and commitment to living the Christian life. A growing class meets the needs of the church as these members get involved in the total ministry of the congregation—more members in classes mean that more people can help others through the church. And a growing class meets the needs of families, giving strength and purpose as all members are nurtured according to ages and interests. Sunday school growth is not an end in itself, rather, growth is a method we use to get more persons committed as followers of Jesus Christ.

THE FIRST STEP: BELIEVE IN GROWTH

If you want your class to grow, you must first believe in growth—that your class MUST, CAN, and WILL grow. When teachers work as growth leaders for their Sunday school classes and are actively involved in outreach, lives are touched.

The teacher's enthusiasm about class growth radiates into the classroom. Once inspired, the students will begin inviting members and relating to one another in an interested, caring manner.

You have seen or heard of classes in which no one seemed to care whether the visitor was welcomed or the unchurched were invited. But if the teacher begins to reach out to these often-overlooked persons, the spirit of nurturing and growth becomes contagious.

WHAT IF WE DON'T GROW?

But what happens when you diligently work toward Sunday school growth, and it just doesn't happen? One woman from a small membership church in a rural area asked, "We'd love to grow, but the fact is that there are very few people in our community to invite." Teachers committed to class growth must constantly stay "charged" even when interest and enthusiasm decline from other class members. The Bible offers us some inspirational words to keep us challenged as Christians for class growth.

1. Persevere.

The challenge of Hebrews 12:1 is this:

*"Let us run
with perseverance
the race
that is set
before us."*

This perseverance involves not giving up in times of class apathy but "hanging in" and continuing to put forth effort until results are seen.

God's time is not always our time. Often we take the attitude of "I want it, and I want it now." God reminds us of the virtue of patience and asks us to wait.

If you have tried every way listed to recruit new members for your class and it still doesn't happen, relax for awhile and focus on nurturing the members you have.

2. Be persistent.

Luke offers guidance for being steadfast in Acts 2:42: "They devoted themselves to the apostles' teaching and fellowship, to the breaking of bread and the prayers."

As a Sunday school teacher, you can help class members feel stability by demonstrating a deep commitment. Such persistence motivates members to believe in a power that moves deeper than the surface enthusiasm of a class. This commitment keeps classes strong, even when the enthusiasm is at a low point. Persistence involves loyalty to what you know in your head and your heart rather than giving in to what you may feel during one low moment.

When your students work at inviting others to class and there are no responses, remind them of this Scripture—of staying devoted to Jesus Christ and his mission.

3. Pray.

The psalmist says, "Evening and morning and at noon I utter my complaint and moan, and he will hear my voice" (Ps. 55:17).

Prayer does change things. In a Sunday school class, prayer can unite the members and can give purpose to a searching group of people. At First United Methodist Church, the teacher of the adult class realized the power of prayer in helping the situation. He began each class session with conversational prayer and kept ongoing prayer lists for the class members. Other members kept the class and its members in their prayers each day. As the group prayed together for new life in their class, they felt a true fellowship again.

Prayer can be that special communication that enables your members to know of God's love and power, even when the enthusiasm for growth is not felt.

4. Recognize possibility.

In Mark 14:36, Jesus prayed, "Abba, Father, for you all things are possible; remove this cup from me; yet, not what I want, but what you want." And Paul teaches in Philippians 4:13,

"I can do everything
God asks me to
with the help of Christ
who gives me
the strength and power." (TLB)

Our Christian faith is a faith of hope. Realizing the possibility and promise in our lives is one of the keys to successful Christian living. The teacher of one class had to rediscover this possibility in her small class.

"We found that the personal dedication of each member to attendance and prayer helped to show the possibility we had as a strong group of Christians," the teacher said. "Even though we haven't had a flood of new visitors, the members became more committed to each other as brothers and sisters in Christ. The exciting part about our growth is that we have activated many of those who had irregular attendance."

Seeing the possibility in your class as it sets goals for growth can be exciting. While you are waiting for growth to occur, classes can channel their energies into mission, work, study, and caring for current members. This awesome power of God is limitless if the members come with an attitude of anticipation.

YOUR CLASS CAN GROW!

Yes, your Sunday school class *can* grow. Growth in the local Sunday school is a necessity and a reality, but it begins with you—the teacher. As you develop a winning attitude for growth, use innovative evangelism tools to reach out to those in your church and community,

GROWING A GREAT SUNDAY SCHOOL CLASS

train your members to become "inviters," and stay creative in the classroom, you will experience growth—both quantitatively and qualitatively—in your class.

Remember the promise of the Scripture found in Job 14:7: "For there is hope for a tree—if it's cut down it sprouts again, and grows tender, new branches" (TLB).

It is our prayer that your class will branch out and bring forth new fruit for Jesus Christ!

In His Service
Bob and Debbie Bruce